MIND
RENOVATION

Dwight J. Olney

MIND RENOVATION

ISBN-13: 978-1-77069-218-3

Printed in Canada.

Word Alive Press
131 Cordite Road, Winnipeg, Manitoba, R3W 1S1
www.wordalivepress.ca

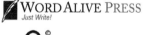

Mixed Sources
Cert no. SW-COC-001271
© 1996 FSC

FSC

Library and Archives Canada Cataloguing in Publication

Olney, Dwight J. (Dwight James), 1960-
    Mind renovation / Dwight J. Olney.

ISBN 978-1-77069-218-3

    1. Thought and thinking--Religious aspects--Christianity.
I. Title.

BV4598.4.O46 2010   248.4   C2010-907888-8

Dedication

This work is respectfully dedicated to my great wife, Jeanette, who lovingly bore my children and continues to bear with me in all my short-comings on the journey.

Contents

Introduction

I refuse to make any more New Year's resolutions. I can't take the disappointment. Despite the sincerity of my intentions, such perennial acts of the will usually fail. Why is that? The human soul consists of three components—mind, heart, and will. The mind is the center of knowledge, reason, and conscience. The heart is the hub of emotions, appetites, and affections. And the will makes choices.

In our natural state, our minds are closed, unenlightened, and blinded, while our hearts are hard towards God. Our wills? Though we may think they are free, our wills are actually prisoners of our hearts and minds. The will obeys what the heart and mind tell it to do. In the Garden of Eden, Eve saw (mind), desired (heart), and then ate (will).

The components of the soul function like a democracy. There are three members that require a majority to execute a decision. The mind and the heart usually vote together and these little monkeys can be quite rascally. The Bible says, *"the human heart and mind are cunning"* (Psalm 64:6). If the will tries to go out there on its own, it gets defeated by the monkeys, two to one. If the will makes a unilateral decision, it's not binding—it doesn't last.

As the calendar year draws to a close, we determine to make better choices in our lives—"I'm going to turn this thing around!" But when we force our wills to do something that the mind and heart do not support, no real change occurs. When our minds are full of purely human thoughts and our hearts are hard and full of wrong appetites, we will not be able to demonstrate a consistent and genuine love for God and for our neighbors (Mark 12:30–31).

We may force our wills to make better decisions, improve our behavior, and follow God more closely, but if the mind and heart are not repaired, the mini revival is short-lived. What we really need to do is address the problem in the right order. Instead of sticking our wills out in front undefended, we need to take care of two renovation projects—a renewed mind and a reformed heart (Ezekiel 36:26). This book stays focused on the need for a mind renovation, leaving others to explore the work of the Holy Spirit in reshaping our hearts and giving us new appetites and desires.

My first book, *Master Mind: Thinking Like God*, presented the notion that improper human behavior often stems from erroneous thinking. I am still thoroughly convinced of this fact. As long as we remain entrenched in our natural human thought patterns, we will struggle to rise above selfishness, nasty habits, and dirty politics. If we want to walk in holiness before God and function fruitfully in his Kingdom, we must make some serious changes in the way we think. We must learn to think like God.

I refer to this transformational necessity as a mind renovation because we need to go beyond simply adding a few biblical truths to what naturally resides in our craniums. Like a typical bathroom or kitchen renovation, the project gets done only through an untidy process of tearing out the old before bringing in the new. This is not a Band-Aid solution. Something drastic and chaotic must happen, despite the fact that we may fool ourselves into thinking otherwise.

Even in home renovations we trick ourselves. Initially, we envision only a few changes, keeping much of the room intact. But once we start tearing things apart, we realize the task is greater than we anticipated. We acknowledge that we are in for a long haul of hard and messy work that will, at times, even be annoying.

God has promised to transform his children into new people by changing the way we think (Romans 12:2), but adopting a divine paradigm requires a great deal of renovation work. Weak and faulty components must be identified and removed from our minds before God's way of thinking can settle in to stay. The two cannot coexist, just as you would never think of keeping an old rusty bath faucet in your shiny new tub.

But unlike home renovations, when we embark on a mind renovation, we may not readily recognize that which is in need of replacement. Everything seems fine. We are comfortable with our usual ways of thinking. We have nursed them from birth and feel at home with them.

But there truly is a problem. Our natural minds are set on earthly things and awash in dirt and debris. So unless we are prepared to study God's Word intensely to discern the divine paradigm, we may never get off the broad path headed for destruction.

Because we are inundated with waves of worldly thoughts from birth, we have multiple misconceptions about God in our thinking and we end up wandering in a host of wrong directions. When we fail to learn how our Creator thinks, we inadvertently say and do many foolish things.

We don't purposely set out to mess up. We all want to live right. And as was presented in *Master Mind*, right living has its most authentic origins in right thinking. But this is not just about mind games, wishful thinking, or the power of positive thought. We cannot change our lives by merely thinking nice thoughts about ourselves and others. We cannot simply will ourselves to be better people by drumming up greater resources of decency and politeness. No, it is far more radical than that. A massive renovation is needed.

Such a renovation can set off a chain reaction. A renewed mind often leads to a softer heart which in turn leads to a properly surrendered will. It's not a magic formula, but our wills more naturally choose properly when the mind and heart are aligned with God's perspective.

If this sounds simple, maybe that's because it is. Ironically, to think like God is actually much simpler than to think like a human. God's thoughts involve simple principles—give, serve, love, forgive, obey. Don't misunderstand me. I said the thoughts of God involve simple principles; they are not simple to embrace, for our human thought patterns make everything in life more convoluted.

The hardest part of learning to think like God is not adopting the new, but rather, unravelling the old. The greatest challenge for us will always be the removal of our messed-up human thinking that is twisted around every synapse of our brains. Limited human thinking impedes us from realizing in our lives the simple truths of the Gospel as well as experiencing true human satisfaction. For this cerebral malady, a mind renovation has been prescribed by the Great Physician.

And so we continue the journey, for that's what it is. Learning to think like God is an ongoing voyage. No discussion of God's thoughts could ever be considered exhaustive. *Master Mind* began the journey. *Mind Renovation* is another step along the way. Like that old house that inspires one renovation project after another, the process of our own mind renovation will, most likely, be an ongoing undertaking until the day we meet the Master face to face, and we *"know everything completely, just as God now knows [us] completely"* (1 Corinthians 12:13).

Chapter 1

"Oops, my infinity is showing."

"Through everything God made, they can clearly see his invisible qualities—his eternal power and divine nature."

~ Romans 1:20

At first glance, it may appear that life is finite—we run out of money, our grandparents rarely live past a hundred, and a man's underwear eventually evaporates. The world advises us to enjoy the here and now, because that is all we have.

Natural human thinking tends to see limits before possibilities, boundaries before infinity. Few people can see beyond what is right before their eyes. History has produced only a lean share of true visionaries. As we enter this world, we naturally assume the limits we see are true limits.

A baby staring at the bars of his crib has trouble envisioning what lies beyond them. The toddler confined to play in the safety of her backyard knows very little about the possibilities just over the fence. The middle school student, though acquiring the ability to think abstractly, struggles to see beyond the walls of his school and the enormous zit in the middle of his forehead. An administrative assistant stuck in her office cubicle for eight hours a day has difficulty picturing a new career outside her box.

We find both distress and comfort within our borders. We become accustomed to the margins that surround us and do not easily see past them. It's no wonder we have so few people really caring about God's existence and his authority over their lives. If we don't stop and look carefully, we may erroneously conclude that God lives out there somewhere, while our world, the supposed 'real' world, is just the finite globe that we can see.

To think like a human is to see the world as more finite than infinite. We are naturally somewhat myopic. We see only restrictive limits and conclude that, if we work hard, perhaps we can master certain accomplishments within those limits and make the most of our tiny existence. Natural human thinking in this post-Nietzsche world deduces that life is about us in a finite sphere; the best we can do is try to find some meaning within the confines of these borders.

To think like God, on the other hand, is to see a bigger picture. To think like God is to look for him everywhere, to recognize his infinite power in many places. God has slipped infinity into every nook and cranny of Creation. And he has done so for our sake, to remind us of him. He wants there to be no confusion for the honest seeker. He wants us to know absolutely that, although invisible, he is indeed present and eternally powerful. Everywhere we look, his infinity is showing. We just need to learn to look properly.

Listen to the words of the Apostle Paul:

> The basic reality of God is plain enough. Open your eyes and there it is! By taking a long and thoughtful look at what God has created, people have always been able to see what their eyes as such can't see: eternal power, for instance, and the mystery of his divine being. So nobody has a good excuse (Romans 1:19–20 MSG).

Paul makes it very clear that God's eternal and divine power is blatantly evident within his Creation. Let's start with the obvious.

One cannot pensively gaze up into the sky on a jet-black night and not feel at least a twinge of eternity. Telescopes have been available since Galileo's time in the early 17th century, but the average person doesn't make much of an effort to investigate outer space. The illuminated sky of the daylight hours is not that impressive, but the star-spangled expanse on a crisp clear night produces a light show rivalling any Hollywood production.

> *The heavens proclaim the glory of God. The skies display his craftsmanship. Day after day they continue to speak; night after night they make him known. They speak without a sound or word; their voice is never heard. Yet their message has gone throughout the earth, and their words to all the world* (Psalm 19:1–4).

Eugene Peterson translates these last sentences in the following manner: *"Their words aren't heard, their voices aren't recorded, but their silence fills the earth: unspoken truth is spoken everywhere"* (19:3–4 MSG). That's awesome—"unspoken truth is spoken everywhere." You cannot hear a sound, but you cannot *not* hear the truth of God's glorious presence.

Perhaps in the pre-Edison era, there was more natural awareness of the infinity of space. Without electricity, people stopped working when the Sun set. There were no big city lights to wash out the glory of the dark night sky. A simpler time made for a simpler examination of the heavens. I'm sure countless peasants and farmers first met their God on an affluently starry night.

And yet today, our scientific knowledge of space is so advanced, we have to deliberately anaesthetize our senses to miss God's infinite greatness as we study the Universe. The Hubble Space Telescope has given us images of the depths of space that are so fantastic, words cannot capture their glory. If you have never done so, you must visit the Hubble Site Gallery at http://hubblesite.org/gallery/. Then you will know why David wrote Psalm 19.

Besides the beauty and majesty of outer space, the scope and depth of the Universe testify to nothing but infinity. There is no perceivable end to our cosmos. Our little ball of rock is one of eight or so planets that orbit in a Solar System that has one star, the Sun. Our Solar System lies within a galaxy housing possibly 200–400 billion stars.[1] Our galaxy is just one of perhaps 130 billion galaxies in the entire Universe.[2] If these estimates are correct, that would mean God has given us at least 50 000 billion billion stars in the Universe. A billion billion is 1 000 000 000 000 000 000. If you can wrap your head around that number, try grasping 50 000 of them.

The naked eye can see only about 5000 of the brightest stars, and most of these would be within 1000 light-years of the Earth. Besides the Sun, the closest star to Earth is a little over four light-years away (i.e. the distance light would travel in four years at about 300 000 km/sec). Who knows how far away the most distant star hangs in space? Recently, the size of the whole known Universe has been approximated to be at least 156 billion light years wide.[3]

These numbers stagger the imagination. But that's good. God deliberately made the Universe so massive, we can never see the end of it. From the days of Adam and Eve to the Hubble and beyond, outer space declares God's eternal and divine power. Astronomers will be without excuse.

But, what if we travel in the other direction? What do we find when we examine those parts of Creation sitting right in front of us.

Initially, it's hard to see God's infinity when we gaze at small things. A grain of table salt seems like just that—a single grain of salt. But if we continually slice that particle of salt in half until we can do it no more, we would have one

---

[1] Cited June 10, 2010 http://www.scientific-web.com/en/Astronomy/
    Galaxies/MilkyWay.html

[2] Cited June 10, 2010 http://astronomy.swin.edu.au/~gmackie/billions.html

[3] Cited June 10, 2010 http://www.space.com/scienceastronomy/
    mystery_monday_040524.html

compound molecule of sodium chloride (NaCl). If we split that molecule, we would have one sodium atom and one chlorine atom.

If we look closer at the sodium atom, we can see that it consists of a nucleus with eleven protons and twelve neutrons, surrounded by eleven electrons. If we isolate one proton within this sodium atom, we see that it too is comprised of even smaller particles of matter known as quarks. Quarks were first theorized in the 1960's but not observed until the 1990's. In the twenty-first century, scientists are proposing that quarks may be made up of even smaller bits of matter. A good theologian would favor this hypothesis. For when we look out into space as far as we can see, we observe eternity; and when we look inside matter as far as we can see, we again witness infinity.

What at first glance appears to be finite is actually eternal. Matter was designed that way by the Creator so we can see his divine nature when we study its inner workings. God has done this for our benefit. He does not want us to be fooled into thinking that his Creation can ever be fully viewed or comprehended.

Besides the infinitesimally miniature size of matter particles, consider the nature of God's building blocks themselves. As far as we can perceive, atomic matter is eternal. It cannot be destroyed; matter can only be altered to take different forms. Again, God's eternal power is evident. Physicists will be without excuse.

But where else has God left his mark of infinity? One of the most obvious locations is, unsurprisingly, mathematics. Caution! If this subject brings back too many painful memories from your childhood, skip ahead a few paragraphs—we'll catch up to you soon.

When we study a Real Number line, we see at least two types of infinity. The arrows on a number line represent the fact that we can never reach its endpoints. There is no limit to the quantity of zeros we can put on the end of a number or after the decimal point in a tiny decimal fraction. But there is also infinity within the number line itself. Pick two numbers close together on the line such as 5.2 and 5.3. Now, pick a number that lies in between these two numbers—5.25, for example. Now, select a number that lies between 5.2 and 5.25—5.247 for example. This process could be continued forever. There is no place where we can reach the bottom. Number lines are infinitely deep. There will always be a smaller quantity in between the two tightest packed numbers conceived by the human mind.

And how about irrational numbers? Irrationals are numbers that cannot be expressed as fractions. They are non-repeating, non-terminating decimals, like pi (π), for instance (3.14159265358979323846...). Pi is an infinite number that is derived by dividing the circumference of a circle by its diameter. Every time you see a circle, you should be reminded of not only the eternal nature of a circle's shape, but also of the infinite character of pi therein. Mathematicians will be without excuse.

Enough math—how about some geology? The age of the Earth has been greatly disputed for many years. Young-Earth Creationists insist that it is about 10 000 years old, while most modern geologists conclude it to be about 4.54 billion.[4] As a teenager, I was greatly interested in Creationist literature and became convinced that the Earth had to be young in order to fit in with biblical chronology. Now that I am older, I am less sure of anything specifically about the origin of the Earth besides the fact that God created it. I will leave the Hebrew scholars to debate the timing and logistics of Creation, but I tend to lean towards an older Earth these days.

Christians should not be threatened by radiometric dating methods that assign an ancient age to the Earth; these methods are not necessarily tools of the devil. What if these dating methods are correct? What if some of the rocks on this planet truly are over four billion years old? Science is merely the

---

[4] Cited February 17, 2009 http://en.wikipedia.org/wiki/Age_of_the_earth

search for truth, and all truth is God's truth. It is silly and insulting for Christians to automatically assume that all scientists are pagans, set on deceiving the world with their false findings. Most scientists enter their fields to learn truth, not to become liars.

Agreed, evolutionary science is incredibly weak; in fact, much of evolutionary research should not even be referred to as 'science'. Ideas like macroevolution and the bizarre mathematical probabilities involved in evolutionary theory place it in the realm of pure speculation, outside the world of true science.

But dating methods that peg the Earth to be ancient, or Big Bang theories that surmise a fourteen-billion-year-old Universe do not have to go hand in hand with evolutionary theory. God could have specially created everything in the Universe over a tremendous period of human time. Why not? He is God, remember? If he took billions of years to prepare my home, that just shows me how much he loves me. If he created everything with the appearance of age in six literal 24-hour days, 6000–10 000 years ago, I'm good with that too.

But I cannot help but ask the question—if God said we are supposed to see infinity when we examine his Creation (e.g. Earth), why would we hunt for evidence of a young Earth? What age of the Earth do you suppose fits best with Romans 1:20?

It seems apparent—God wants us to spot his infinity wherever we look. When I walk on the sands of a beach, I try to imagine the incalculable number of grains that must exist on the entire surface of the planet. When I study biology, I marvel at the 60–100 trillion cells in the human body and the 100 billion neurons that form the countless synapse connections in the human brain. When I ponder meteorology, I am reminded of the eternal flow of the jet streams that continually bring us our changing weather patterns. When I look at the ocean, I see 1.5 billion cubic kilometers of water, the eternal lapping of waves on its shores, and the infinite supply of plankton that is perpetually created to feed trillions of sea creatures.

And these casual observations do not take into consideration the divine demonstrations of God's power in massive waterfalls, avalanches, earthquakes, volcanoes, hurricanes, tides, tornadoes, and icebergs.

Let's go in another direction. Even inventions birthed from human imagination in the last half century point to an infinitely powerful divine Maker. Since we are created in God's image, we share some of his characteristics. Hints of God's eternal power show up in our own creations.

Consider the integrated circuit, the heart and soul of all modern electronic devices. Calculators execute complex algorithmic computations in a millisecond. DLP television technology uses millions of computer-controlled micromirrors to produce its TV image, each mirror being one-fifth the width of a human hair.

In automobile engines, computer chips in coordination with dozens of electronic sensors perform millions of calculations each second, including looking up values in tables and calculating the results of long equations to decide the best spark timing or how long a fuel injector should stay open.[5]

The highest level of sophisticated microchip technology is exhibited in the microprocessor, the most complex manufactured product on Earth. The transistors in a microprocessor can execute hundreds of millions of instructions per second. In comparison to regular human experience and natural processing abilities, these numbers are as good as infinity.

And speaking of infinity, how about nanotechnology—countless molecular-sized machines designed to perform cleaning, medicinal, environmental, and manufacturing functions, all at the atomic level? Where will this field take us in our exposure to the infinite?

---

[5] Cited February 17, 2009 http://auto.howstuffworks.com/
car-computer1.htm

Even when we use our World Wide Web search engine technology, it seems like we are experiencing a brush with infinity. Google just found me 1.42 billion websites containing the word 'love', all within 14/100 of a second. (Searched on June 10, 2010)

And then there are the mesmerizing figures involved in computer storage itself. We are all too familiar with finger-sized flash drives holding hundreds of billions of bytes. We marvel at how data storage currency has changed from kilobytes to megabytes to gigabytes to terabytes. In 2007, scientists "built a working memory chip that is roughly the size of a white blood cell—about 1/2000th of an inch on a side."[6]

And now, with serendipitous discoveries emerging from nanotechnology such as the fabrication of memristors, future storage technology will have chips that can store thousands of times more information than anything today.[7]

Wow!

A wise man once wrote: *"God has made everything beautiful for its own time. He has planted eternity in the human heart, but even so, people cannot see the whole scope of God's work from beginning to end"* (Ecclesiastes 3:11). Although we will never fully grasp infinity this side of Heaven, God has given us a notion of eternity in our hearts. When we deliberately take note of the infinite nature of things around us, something right and true rings in the very core of our being. We connect with the Almighty.

God has placed the impression of eternity in our hearts. However, Satan wants to take it away. Ironically, supernatural demonic forces trick us into seeing this world as entirely natural and finite so that we ignore God. When we open ourselves to demonic influence and when we lose ourselves in

---

[6] Cited June 10, 2010 at http://www.nytimes.com/2007/01/24/science/24cnd-chip.html?ex=1327294800&en=92577015d518371a&ei=5088&partner=rssnyt&emc=rss

[7] Cited February 21, 2009 at http://www.nanovip.com/node/53375

sin, we also lose our ability to clearly see the eternal God. We don't hate him; we become more finite, and we grow to be more apathetic to his presence and to what his eternal power can do in our lives.

Opportunities to witness infinity are everywhere— astronomy, geology, atomic theory, biology, mathematics, meteorology, oceanography—even within human inventions and the yearnings of the human heart.

If we take the time to look, we will be inundated with constant reminders of God's eternal power and presence. So, there will be no excuse for anyone. On the Day of Judgment, regardless of any other forms of divine revelation, Creation alone will sufficiently testify against the willful heart that maintains innocence by ignorance or that unabashedly proclaims "There is no God!" All of the Universe will rise up with one voice and pronounce the unrepentant heart to be "Guilty!"

God is telling us, "Pay attention, my infinity is showing."

DISCUSSION QUESTIONS

1. Why do you think God made the Universe so incredibly massive?

2. What fields of study clearly showcase God's infinite and eternal power?

3. Give an example of something that appears finite but is actually infinite.

4. What does it mean to live life with a finite perspective?

5. How are our lives impacted by having a more infinite perspective of all Creation?

6. How does Romans 1:20 relate to the age of the Earth debate?

7. How do human inventions point to God's infinite power?

8. With all the evidence around us displaying infinity, why does the world still have such a finite mindset?

Chapter 2

"My son's name ticks off a lot of people."

"If the world hates you, keep in mind that it hated me first. They will treat you this way because of my name."

~ John 15:18, 21

There is a lot of power in a name.

The mere mention of Hitler, Stalin, Gandhi, Mother Teresa, Toyota, or Rolex evokes various emotional responses. Commanding names conjure up feelings of fear, respect, or trust. Good or bad, reputation and name are inseparable. *No Name* brands in the supermarket lack curb appeal—people are uneasy or bored buying a product that lacks a flashy label.

Every day we discern the value of products or opinions based on the name associated with them. When Warren Buffett tells us to buy, we should probably buy. When Bob Buffett, our barber, tells us to sell, we might want to do a little more research.

Each of our names carries a particular status or standing depending on what we have done with our lives. Some people work hard to establish authoritative names in order to exert influence over others. Some are content to keep their names non-descript. Regardless of what we try to make of our names, the most powerful and evocative name in history is Jesus Christ.

Speaking of him, the Scriptures say, *"There is salvation in no one else! God has given no other name under heaven by which we must be saved"* (Acts 4:12). The God of the Universe has declared that if we want to be made right before him, we must come through that name—Jesus. Based on this fact, and upon his life record of incredible goodness, kindness, and miracle-working power, the name of Jesus should stir up love, adoration, and worship.

Not so. It is obvious that the name of Jesus induces far more negative responses than positive. It's okay to believe in God. But tell people you are a follower of Jesus Christ and they are immediately offended, or at least uncomfortable. Why does our Savior's name make people angry?

Consider what happens when some people make up their minds to start a spiritual journey. After chasing all that is worldly and tempting to their fleshly desires, they become fed up with the drag of materialism and the sameness of sin. They then decide to 'get a little religion' in their lives. More and more, they start to incorporate 'God' into their speech and persona. If this is as far as they go, they will not face much opposition because a vague association with 'God' doesn't ruffle too many feathers.

'God' is not as offensive as 'Jesus'. Most people in the world 'believe in God', but that phrase can mean many things. People talk about believing or not believing in God as if it were an inconsequential choice like taking cream and sugar in their coffee or drinking it black.

Some people say they believe in God, but it doesn't impact their lives. Belief in God can be fairly undemanding when they formulate their own version of him. Bits and pieces of God's character and commands are selected like items off a buffet table. These people do whatever they please, thinking a token acknowledgement of the 'Big Guy Upstairs' assures them of a trip to Heaven.

Other people's belief in God consists of working hard to fulfill many rituals of their man-made religions. As long as they appear sincere and dedicated, their religious zeal stirs up little emotion in others. But as soon as Jesus' name is brought into the picture, people get their backs up.

This should not surprise us. The New Testament often speaks of true Christian believers suffering because of their association with Christ. Jesus warned his disciples, *"If the world hates you, keep in mind that it hated me first...If they persecuted me, they will persecute you also...They will treat you this way because of my name"* (John 15:18–21 NIV).

Speaking of future believers in the end times, Jesus said, *"...they will lay hands on you and persecute you...all on account of my name...You will be betrayed even by parents, brothers, relatives and friends, and they will put some of you to death. All men will hate you because of me"* (Luke 21:12, 16–17 NIV).

Apostles Peter and Paul spoke regularly of this hatred for Christians as being part of the package of following Jesus: *"Everyone who wants to live a godly life in Christ Jesus will suffer persecution"* (2 Timothy 3:12). They referred to this persecution as a calling and a privilege. *"To this you were called, because Christ suffered for you, leaving you an example, that you should follow in his steps"* (1 Peter 2:21 NIV). *"For you have been given not only the privilege of trusting in Christ but also the privilege of suffering for him"* (Philippians 1:29).

Peter and Paul even spoke of our suffering with Christ as a partnership (1 Peter 4:13) and a fellowship (Philippians 3:10 NIV).

Paul, in particular, was very familiar with this concept of the name of Jesus making people irate. He himself was once inflamed with anti-Christian ferocity. Speaking of his life before Christ saved him, he said, *"I used to blaspheme the name of Christ. In my insolence, I persecuted his people"* (1 Timothy 1:13). But when Christ revealed himself to Paul on the road to Damascus, the Lord's message for the new convert was, *"I will show him how much he must suffer for my name's sake"* (Acts 9:16).

So, the natural human tendency is to be anti-Christ. Religious gestures may bring God loosely into the picture of our lives, but thinking like God involves a commitment of full surrender to Jesus Christ. We need to take seriously God's view of his son and embrace the persecution that accompanies such a decision.

God the Father says Jesus is the head of everything, the Creator and sustainer of all things both seen and unseen (Colossians 1:16–17). *"He is the beginning, supreme over all who rise from the dead. So he is first in everything"* (Colossians 1:18). The Book of Ephesians says,

> *[God]...raised Christ from the dead and seated him in the place of honor at God's right hand in the heavenly realms. Now he is far above any ruler or authority or power or leader or anything else—not only in this world but also in the world to come. God has put all things under the authority of Christ and has made him head over all things for the benefit of the church* (1:20–22).

Because of his supremacy, God demands that all mankind and every spiritual being bow before him and submit to his authority.

> *Therefore, God elevated him to the place of highest honor and gave him the name above all other names, that at the name of Jesus every knee should bow, in heaven and on earth and under the earth, and every tongue confess that Jesus Christ is Lord, to the glory of God the Father* (Philippians 2:9–11).

The pre-eminence of Christ is evident throughout the Scriptures. His name is the source of all life (John 20:31), healing (Acts 3:6, 4:10), and forgiveness of sins (Acts 2:38). When we call on the name of the Lord Jesus, we can be cleansed, made holy, and justified before God (1 Corinthians 6:11). Demons were cast out in the name of Jesus (Acts 16:18) and his name was always associated with the Good News of the Kingdom of God (Acts 8:12).

Christian believers are exhorted to assemble in the name of the Lord Jesus (1 Corinthians 5:4) and to always give thanks to God in the Son's name (Ephesians 5:20). In fact, the name of Jesus should be the central theme of everything we do: *"And whatever you do, whether in word or deed, do it all in the name of the Lord Jesus, giving thanks to God the Father through him"* (Colossians 3:17 NIV).

The Apostle Paul preached fearlessly in the name of Jesus (Acts 9:27), risked his life for the cause (Acts 15:26), and openly confessed that he was ready to die for that name (Acts 21:13). His ongoing prayer for the people he discipled was that *"the name of our Lord Jesus will be honored because of the way you live"* (2 Thessalonians 1:12).

The writer of Hebrews tells his readers to *"offer through Jesus a continual sacrifice of praise to God, proclaiming our allegiance to his name"* (Hebrews 13:15). Notice that our allegiance to the name of Jesus is referred to as a sacrifice of praise. A sacrifice costs the worshiper something. If we are not feeling that cost, perhaps we are not being vocal enough about our commitment to his name.

In the Book of Revelation, special honor is given to the churches who *"have persevered and have endured hardships for my name, and have not grown weary"* (2:3 NIV) and for those who *"have kept my word and have not denied my name"* (3:8 NIV).

So, we come back to the question raised earlier—what is it about the name of Jesus that makes people so uncomfortable and even angry?

Many things.

First of all, Jesus is messy. There's blood involved. An abhorrent cross designed for killing criminals stands as the focal point of the salvation story. The Savior's flesh is torn to shreds for public display, not what we'd envision for the protagonist in the saga of mankind's deliverance.

And there's a lot of surrender involved. Following Jesus is hard. He requires that we make a complete commitment. If we water down the true meaning of the word believe, we can 'sort of believe' in God, but we cannot 'sort of follow' Christ. It's all or nothing. He calls us to a new life that is radically different than our old one. If you deem yourself as one who is sitting on the fence regarding a pledge to Christ, you most assuredly have not made one. This demanding level of personal abandonment and loyalty to Jesus is what turns off an earthly mind.

And his standards are high. If you don't believe me, check out the Sermon on the Mount recorded in Matthew 5–7. To be associated with the name of Jesus means we need to take things more seriously than most people want to. It also implies a separation from the world that makes people think Christians are full of themselves. Jesus said to his followers, *"The world would love you as one of its own if you belonged to it, but you are no longer part of the world. I chose you to come out of the world, so it hates you"* (John 15:19).

Following Christ also involves humility. Instead of finding our own way to God, we need to bow down, admit our weakness, and acknowledge our need for a Savior. Pursuing Christ is a humbling experience where we are forced to lay our lives bare before him and plead for his blood to cleanse us.

And, of course, there is the exclusivity aspect that people find so offensive. Jesus said, *"You can enter God's Kingdom only through the narrow gate. The highway to hell is broad, and its gate is wide for the many who choose that way"* (Matthew 7:13). He also said, *"I am the way, the truth, and the life. No one can come to the Father except through me"* (John 14:6). These claims subject followers of Christ to a judgment of being arrogant and presumptuous.

Certainly, there are Christians who taint the name of the Savior by their hypocritical behavior. Many honest seekers have been turned away from Christ because of the confusion caused by watching a false believer live a life with little integrity. But Jesus himself was blameless.

Throughout his ministry, he showed time and time again just how much he truly loved people, especially the bad ones. Jesus' ministry was a showcase of wonderful acts of goodness. Some days he spent the entire day healing people's diseases, and then fed them supper (Matthew 14:13–21). People who suffered for many years were delivered from paralyzing and debilitating sicknesses and demon possession.

And yet, the religious leaders of first century Palestine were obsessed with an uncharacteristic hatred for him. On more than one occasion, Jesus' healings on the Sabbath threw the Jewish leaders into a horrible rage (Luke 6:6–11; 13:10–17). Strangely, these religious teachers had no compassion for those poor souls who were being delivered from bondage.

The anger of his enemies was psychotic. It made no sense. He healed a woman of a horrible disease that had tormented her for eighteen years—so they wanted to kill him? He only desired to bring good things to the lives of needy people. But because his ministry upset the religious establishment, they became fanatical about killing him. A plan was set in motion that would lead to his crucifixion.

And one of the most bizarre aspects of the crucifixion is how quickly the people of Jerusalem turned on Jesus. The hatred displayed by the Jewish mob at Christ's trial was absurd. Pilate offered to free Jesus as a gesture of Roman goodwill because they were in the middle of the Jewish Passover feast. But the crowd cried for the release of Barabbas, a convicted felon guilty of murder and insurrection. Get this—the general population preferred to have a killer back on the streets rather than Jesus. The Son of God, who came to bring us abundant life, was assailed with livid shouts of "Crucify him!" How incredulous and ridiculous!

Despite the incongruity of it all, the religious establishment eventually got their way—the God-man, Jesus, was put to death. But the power of God raised him back to life and took him to Heaven.

It didn't take long after Christ's ascension for the hatred of his name to re-surface. The disciples began to preach to large crowds of people interested in the story of Jesus. When hauled before courts and councils, Christ's followers were never rebuked for doing anything evil; they were just specifically *"commanded never again to speak or teach in the name of Jesus"* (Acts 4:18; 5:40). Again, there was no praising God for his good work or rejoicing over the alleviation of suffering, just inane hatred for the precious name of Jesus.

Even today, there continues to exist this irrational and illogical revulsion towards the name of Jesus and all who take seriously his claims on their lives. If we want to think like God, we cannot escape this criticism. God has made Jesus pre-eminent and has made salvation exclusive. He has the right to do so because he is God. To truly think like God will continually direct our focus and devotion on Jesus, his beloved son. This focus will automatically draw a negative reaction from a worldly system that cannot stand his name.

But this is good news, because it means we're on the right path. It means we're being identified with Christ and his sufferings. And there is a special place of honor for those who endure persecution for following Christ.

Jesus' disciples were never discouraged by the rough treatment that accompanied being associated with Christ's name. Rather, *"the apostles left the high council rejoicing that God had counted them worthy to suffer disgrace for the name of Jesus"* (Acts 5:41). Jesus had prepared his followers for this mistreatment. He had said to them earlier, *"Blessed are you when people insult you, persecute you and falsely say all kinds of evil against you because of me"* (Matthew 5:11). Siding with the name of Christ has the potential to bring more than just anger our way—we may be deliberately left out, ridiculed, and cursed.

If we are not prepared for that level of humiliation, we are not ready to follow Christ. And as I suggested earlier, if we are not experiencing any contempt on account of our faith, perhaps we are not holding the name of Jesus high enough for anyone to notice. Boldly proclaiming the name of Jesus summons Satan's hatred and marks us as a target. Our enemy and the worldly system he runs cannot stomach Christ's supremacy.

> *So be happy when you are insulted for being a Christian, for then the glorious Spirit of God rests upon you. If you suffer, however, it must not be for murder, stealing, making trouble, or prying into other people's affairs. But it is no shame to suffer for being a Christian. Praise God for the privilege of being called by his name!* (1 Peter 4:14–16)

To think like God, we must not back down from confidently declaring the name of Jesus, for there is salvation in none other. May we, like Paul, *"preach Christ"* (Colossians 1:28 MSG) in all that we do and say. The time for shyness is past. Don't be brash or ill-mannered, but be brave. For *"what blessings await you when people hate you and exclude you and mock you and curse you as evil because you follow the Son of Man"* (Luke 6:22).

God is warning us today—if you ride with my son, some folks are going to hate you. The name of Jesus ticks off a lot of people. But his name is the key to our salvation, the power of our deliverance, and the hope of our eternal glory.

DISCUSSION QUESTIONS

1. What's the difference between 'believing in God' and 'following Jesus'?

2. Why is the name of Jesus so offensive?

3. What is so significant about the name of Jesus according to the biblical writers?

4. It's hard for the human mind to think of persecution as a good thing. What are some words or phrases in Scripture that are associated with suffering for Christ?

5. The responses Jesus received to his ministry were ironic. Explain.

6. Practically speaking, what does it mean to boldly proclaim the name of Jesus?

7. Is it possible to boldly proclaim the name of Jesus without experiencing the world's contempt?

8. Can Christians use shyness as an excuse for not vocally declaring the significance of Jesus in their lives?

Chapter 3

"True greatness serves."

"Whoever wants to become great among you must be your servant."

~ Mark 10:43 NIV

Everyone wants to have a great future. Everyone desires their life to be great. But what does it mean to be great? What does it mean to execute a great achievement? Several historical figures have had the title affixed to their name—Alexander, Peter, and Catherine, just to name a few.

If you study enough history, you might conclude that to earn this designation you need to kill a lot of people or accumulate a lot of territory. But besides military conquest, there have been many accomplishments in the past that we consider to be great.

In science, the invention of the telescope and the discovery of black holes were astounding achievements. In technology, the printing press and the lunar module were amazing creations. In medical history, one of the greatest moments was the nineteenth century discovery that more people die from the invisible bacteria on a scalpel than from the poor surgical skill of an untrained doctor. In sports, no one will ever reproduce the hockey numbers posted by 'The Great One' or re-create better highlight reels than Michael Jordan. In music, Handel's composition of *The Messiah* is a great masterpiece that may never be surpassed. And now, in the

Information Age, ingenious and innovative thinkers have amassed large fortunes through their great ideas that have transformed the way we work, live, and play—men like Steve Jobs, Bill Gates, and the creators of Google and Facebook.

History is full of great events. The world has pronounced many people and many accomplishments as great. But usually such acknowledgements are reserved for people who realize great feats that bring abundant wealth and/or glory to themselves.

Yet in the twentieth century, we started to see a change. There began a public acknowledgement that great people may not just be those individuals who live off the wealth of their great triumphs in luxurious mansions. Humanitarian self-sacrificing servants such as Gandhi, Billy Graham, and Mother Teresa began to receive their due recognition and admiration, even though they have never been showcased on *Lifestyles of the Rich and Famous*. Such a sociological transformation is good, for it reflects something closer to the truth about genuine greatness, the kind Jesus talked about.

On more than one occasion, Jesus was given the opportunity to discuss greatness since his disciples loved to bring up the topic. They were prone to quarrel amongst themselves regarding who was the greatest, or who would end up with positions of higher authority in the Kingdom of God. Probably the most bizarre of such occurrences was the debate the disciples held during the Last Supper. Listen to Luke's account of this fascinating episode as recorded in the twenty-second chapter of his Gospel:

> *Within minutes they were bickering over who of them would end up the greatest. But Jesus intervened: "Kings like to throw their weight around and people in authority like to give themselves fancy titles. It's not going to be that way with you. Let the senior among you become like the junior; let the leader act the part of the servant. Who would you rather be: the one who eats the dinner or the one who serves the dinner? You'd rather eat and be served, right?*

But I've taken my place among you as the one who serves"
(Luke 22:24–27).

The essence of Jesus' teaching is that true greatness
serves. Most people in the world don't naturally gravitate to
this perspective, but it is at the core of God's thinking. There
are a lot of talented people in the world, but the measure of
true greatness in the annals of eternity is the capacity of the
heart to humble itself and serve others. It consists of the ability
to be unselfish, to see the needs and desires of others as more
important than our own, no matter who we are.

Regardless of our strength, speed, intelligence, humor,
creativity, cleverness, wit, or musical ability, we must
establish a mindset that leads us to a lifestyle of unselfish
giving, serving the Lord and serving our fellow man. To be a
great person, we need to see every opportunity in life as a
chance to make a contribution to the Kingdom of God,
repeatedly depositing something good into the lives of others.

Mankind's resistance to this servant paradigm is clearly
seen in our inclination to go vertical rather than horizontal.
Instead of moving outwards horizontally in service toward
others, we are constantly aiming for something higher,
something taller. Somehow the height of our achievement is
supposedly a reflection of our greatness.

It doesn't take much coaxing to get man to try to go high.
Little children reveal that human propensity from their earliest
days, seeing how high they can climb up that tree in the
backyard. Mountain climbers conquering Everest display the
same fervor. The higher you go, the greater the esteem. This
doesn't just apply to trees and mountains, but also to career
aspirations. We strive to ascend the corporate ladder to earn
higher financial remuneration and attain greater regard. To the
human mind, higher always seems better, especially if there is
a building involved.

We saw this in the story of the Tower of Babel.
Remember their dialogue? *"Come, let's build a great city for
ourselves with a tower that reaches into the sky. This will*

make us famous and keep us from being scattered all over the world" (Genesis 11:4). They concluded that a tall tower would make them great people, maybe even elevate them to celebrity status. Because they were so off-task from the real purpose of life, God put the kibosh on their project with a little gift of tongues.

But this proclivity for vertical human achievement and its accompanying arrogance continued throughout history, making a strong showing in the Middle Ages with its Gothic cathedral building competitions. Through the use of the pointed arch, the ribbed vault, and flying buttresses to support the weight of the building, astounding new architectural heights were achieved. Gothic cathedrals dwarfed their Romanesque predecessors and a town or bishop's pride was often connected with the height of its cathedral. The church, the one organization in the world that should have known better, ignored Christ's command to serve, and became preoccupied with majestic structural silliness that resulted in civic unrest, political scheming, oppressive taxation, and even murder. Their obsession also led to the deaths of church builders and parishioners who occasionally became victims of powerful men's misguided quests for greatness when overzealous structures came crashing down on their heads (e.g. Beauvais Cathedral in 1284).

This pursuit of vertical enormity continues to this day with our penchant for immense skyscrapers. First it was the Eiffel Tower, then the Empire State Building, the World Trade Center, the Sears Tower, the CN Tower, and now United Arab Emirates' Burj Dubai with its title-holding height of 2684 feet. And the race continues as others plan to surpass Dubai's mind-boggling penetration of the sky.

This frenzied construction skyward is a clear indication of our compulsion for vertical grandeur, for trophies of human pride and achievement, maybe even our quest for deity. We want to be like God, but in our own styling. In contrast to this infatuation with a vertical rush, God wants us to be preoccupied with going horizontal, serving our fellow man in ever-increasing concentric circles. When it's time, when his plan is complete, we will go vertical—big time! The rapture of the church at Christ's return will be the ultimate vertical rush. But for now, to the divine mind, higher is not nearly as significant as wider.

This encouragement to move outward to serve others is clearly evident in the Scriptures. As we read earlier in Luke's gospel, Jesus wanted his closest friends to understand that service is the highest possible calling in human relations. He not only talked about it, he demonstrated it in hopes that they would mimic him.

The reality is this—we all either serve God and others or we serve ourselves and sin. The Apostle Paul told us straight up,

> *Do not let any part of your body become an instrument of evil to serve sin. Instead, give yourselves completely to God, for you were dead, but now you have new life. So use your whole body as an instrument to do what is right for the glory of God* (Romans 6:13).

"Serve the Lord enthusiastically", he wrote later on in the same letter (Romans 12:11). To the church at Galatia he said,

> *For you have been called to live in freedom, my brothers and sisters. But don't use your freedom to satisfy your sinful nature. Instead, use your freedom to serve one another in love* (Galatians 5:13).

The Apostle Peter joined in: *"And all of you, serve each other in humility, for God opposes the proud but favors the humble"* (1 Peter 5:5). Regarding the abilities that God gives his children to operate within his church, Peter reminded us that these talents need to be exercised with meekness, considering how we can bless others as opposed to just showing off. *"God has given each of you a gift from his great variety of spiritual gifts. Use them well to serve one another"* (1 Peter 4:10).

So, it seems like the point of our lives is to serve. The servant-minded follower of Christ is thinking like God. Service is not a consolation for the weak or some sort of leftover option for losers. It is the modus operandi of winners. Listen to Christ's discussion of his future return to Earth as recorded in Luke 12. Notice how he referred to the winners in this story as waiting servants. And he drew attention to the aspect of readiness as earning special reward:

The servants who are ready and waiting for his return will be rewarded. I tell you the truth, he himself will seat them, put on an apron, and serve them as they sit and eat! He may come in the middle of the night or just before dawn. But whenever he comes, he will reward the servants who are ready (Luke 12:37–38).

But servanthood does not imply mediocrity. It's wonderful when a follower of Jesus is also renowned in their particular field. Christians who are successful in their spheres of influence can have a powerful impact for the Kingdom of God. This world needs great Christian athletes, doctors, and lawyers. It needs great Christian marine biologists, computer programmers as well as great Christian plumbers, electricians, and administrative assistants. This world also needs great Christian parents with the skill and compassion to raise up the next generation to love the Lord.

We need to figure out what interests us and then pursue excellence in that field. Show the world what it is like to be a Christian who is skillful in his/her domain. But as we strive for greatness, in a professional field or politics or as a homemaker, remember the words of Jesus—true greatness serves.

And speaking of greatness, consider carefully the one who was talking here. This advocate and example of humble service is the Son of God, the very divine being who created the Universe and walked a life of sinless perfection as a man on Earth. And he stood before a bunch of fishermen and social disregards, and said: *"I have taken my place among you as one who serves"* (Luke 22:27). The very Son of God, the one who holds all of Creation together by the power of his word, the one who would carry a heavy beam to Golgotha and sacrifice his life for the sin of all mankind, this is the God-man of inexpressible greatness, standing before very ordinary men saying, "You know who I am, yet I am serving you." What irony! What incongruity! The truth of the matter is this—the disciples should have been serving Jesus. They should have been falling all over each other, fighting for the chance to wait on their Master hand and foot. Instead, they were fighting each other over who was the best.

Again, this ongoing greatness debate amongst the disciples was particularly odd at the Last Supper. In John's account of the story, he explained how Jesus started the evening by washing the disciples' dirty feet. Such a foot washing custom was necessary in those days because they ate lying down, exposing their feet to the other guests. And it was the job of the lowest slave in the household to do this menial task.

And yet we had Jesus, the Son of God, their Master and Commander, washing *their* feet before the meal. How humbling, how humiliating for the Lord, the Teacher, to be doing the dirty work of a servant? And then they had the audacity to argue between themselves who was the greatest? Could they have missed the mark any more blatantly?

I hope we are not as slow as these guys to learn from the teaching and example of Jesus that true greatness serves. Listen to Mark's version of Jesus' rebuke to his bickering disciples:

You know that the rulers in this world lord it over their people, and officials flaunt their authority over those under them. But among you it will be different. Whoever wants to be a leader among you must be your servant, and whoever wants to be first among you must be the slave of everyone else. For even the Son of Man came not to be served but to

serve others and to give his life as a ransom for many
(Mark 10:42–45).

Shortly into Christ's ministry, John the Baptist was
murdered. This event was tragic for many, but especially for
Jesus because John was his cousin and boyhood friend. After
hearing of the news, Jesus attempted to get away and procure
some grieving space. Matthew wrote,

> *As soon as Jesus heard the news, he left in a boat to a
> remote area to be alone. But the crowds heard where he
> was headed and followed on foot from many towns. Jesus
> saw the huge crowd as he stepped from the boat, and he
> had compassion on them and healed their sick* (Matthew
> 14:13–14).

Even though the most human response would have been
to tell the crowd to go home because Jesus was emotionally
hurting, the Scripture says he felt compassion for them, and
served their needs first.

According to Jesus, service is the highest calling, the only
one that has true and lasting significance. Everything else will
eventually diminish to its true size. It's time we abandon petty
human thoughts of personal aggrandizement and adopt God's
recipe for a truly great future, both here on Earth and into
eternity. Only then will there be less need for words to spread
the Gospel, for the difference between us and the self-seeking,
status-conscious world will be abundantly clear.

DISCUSSION QUESTIONS

1. Traditionally, how has humanity defined greatness?

2. How did this perception begin to change in the late 20th century?

3. What was Jesus' response to his disciples' constant bickering about human greatness?

4. Illustrate how our desire for human glory is reflected in our tendency to "go vertical."

5. What do Paul and Peter have to say about this matter of servanthood?

6. Is it still okay as a Christian to want to be great in your earthly endeavors? Explain.

7. Describe the irony of the disciples' behaviour at the Last Supper.

8. List several ways Jesus personally exemplified the principle that true greatness serves.

Chapter 4

"I'm looking for a few good words."

"God's in charge, not you—the less you speak, the better."

~ Ecclesiastes 5:2 MSG

To put it succinctly, we talk too much. Even though our ears outnumber our mouths two to one, humans have a proclivity for verbiage. For many of us, the temptation to dominate a conversation is overwhelmingly delicious.

And it gets worse when we're nervous, insecure, or unsure of ourselves. Embarrassment escalates when we are completely clueless about the topic at hand; instead of admitting that we don't know what we're talking about, we start throwing out darts, hoping that some of them might actually hit the target. Sometimes, the less we know, the more we talk.

We say too much in almost every situation. When people ask us questions, we often give far more than what they requested or require. We wax on, just in case someone in the audience is slightly interested in whatever else we may know about the subject matter.

When people are hurting or find themselves in tough situations, we, yet again, say too much. We chatter on, oblivious to the fact that we may be making things worse by our abundance of babble.

The behavior of the three friends in the biblical story of Job is a good example. When they came to visit Job in the midst of his distress, they respectfully refrained from speaking for the first seven days, but then their human nature kicked in. No longer able to contain themselves, they burst forth into an extended series of dueling diatribes that totally frustrated and discouraged their friend. Once they got going, Job could not shut them up.

> *I have heard all this before. What miserable comforters you are! Won't you ever stop blowing hot air? What makes you keep on talking? I could say the same things if you were in my place. I could spout off criticism and shake my head at you. But if it were me, I would encourage you. I would try to take away your grief* (Job 16:2–5).

People with a reputation for copious communication create more irritation than enjoyment. When they enter the room, bystanders cringe at the thought of the impending flow of vocabulary about to gush forth. Like rising water in a plugged toilet, it's only a matter of time before a superfluity of words starts to spill over.

Yes, as humans we have a tendency to talk too much, even in a chapter about talking too much.

God, on the other hand, is a person of few words. *"Let there be light"* (Genesis 1:3). *"Where are you?"* (Genesis 3:9) *"I AM WHO I AM"* (Exodus 3:14). You can't be much more direct or to the point than the pithy declarations of the Ten Commandments. God does not beat around the bush.

Humans are far too wordy for God and for their own good. Earnest and genuine followers of the Lord even fall into the trap of being too verbose as they make their way into his presence. The author of Ecclesiastes gives the sincere worshiper a simple exhortation:

> *As you enter the house of God, keep your ears open and your mouth shut. It is evil to make mindless offerings to*

God. Don't make rash promises, and don't be hasty in bringing matters before God. After all, God is in heaven, and you are here on earth. So let your words be few. Too much activity gives you restless dreams; too many words make you a fool (Ecclesiastes 5:1–3).

Approaching God is a delicate matter. We must not blather on incessantly and we must think carefully about what we say, exercising our words sparingly. Impulsive promises are bad. When we come before God, our first priority should be to listen. The less we open our mouths, the better chance we have of not looking like a fool.

Jesus reiterated this principle in the Sermon on the Mount:

When you pray, don't babble on and on as people of other religions do. They think their prayers are answered merely by repeating their words again and again. Don't be like them, for your Father knows exactly what you need even before you ask him! (Matthew 6:7–8)

Repetitious words don't impress God. He's just looking for a few good ones. That's why Jesus followed up his teaching in Matthew 6 with an example of how to pray. The Lord's Prayer is the antidote to excess lexis; it includes six simple principles, all that is necessary to talk meaningfully with God.

It starts with reverence for our Heavenly Father's name. It continues with a plea for God's Kingdom to come, and his will to be done on Earth just like it's already being done in Heaven. The prayer then concludes with three requests—sustenance, forgiveness of sins, and deliverance from evil. That's it.

God knows what we need before we open our mouths. Prayer is not the act of bringing God up to speed on pressing matters. He doesn't need to tune into our news channel. Rather, prayer is the act of acknowledging the Most Holy One, and submitting to his authority. It is the habit of bowing humbly before him and aligning all our thoughts, emotions, decisions, and desires under his will. We would realize greater effectiveness in our personal prayer life if we listened more and spoke less.

Less is always more. The best Old Testament example of this is the prayer showdown between Elijah and the 450 prophets of Baal. The line-ups were assembled on Mount Carmel—Team Baal vs. Team Yahweh. The challenge was to prepare an oxen offering and see which god would answer by sending down fire from Heaven to consume the sacrifice.

The story is well known. The 450 prophets of Baal cried out with many words for hours as they leaped about the altar. They wept and flailed, and even sliced their skin until the blood gushed out. Think about this. How many words did they actually offer up to Baal? Four hundred and fifty preachers times eight hours of sermons? That's a lot of words, millions. But all their enormous effort was to no avail. Elijah must have had fun teasing them.

Contrast their excessive chatter fest with the simple prayer of Elijah. Once his sacrifice was prepared and doused with twelve pitchers of water, he prayed:

> *O Lord, God of Abraham, Isaac, and Jacob, prove today that you are God in Israel and that I am your servant. Prove that I have done all this at your command. O Lord, answer me! Answer me so these people will know that you, O Lord, are God and that you have brought them back to yourself* (1 Kings 18:36–37).

So, with a few dozen words, the oxen, the wood, the altar, and even the water were all consumed by fire from Heaven. Pagans can offer up all the innumerable chants they want to their non-existent gods, but the one true God of the Universe needs only a few good words to be moved to accomplish his plans—a few good words, honestly delivered from a sincere and surrendered heart.

When we approach our Heavenly Father, he wants few words. This same minimalist philosophy also works well in our relationships. Proverbs 10:19 says, *"Too much talk leads to sin.*

Be sensible and keep your mouth shut." It's inevitable—when there are too many words, transgression in unavoidable. Think about how many times you could have avoided offending someone if you would have just stopped moving your lips a little earlier.

There is so much power in that hunk of flesh behind our teeth. Power for good—*"The right word at the right time is like precious gold set in silver"* (Proverbs 25:11). And power for bad—*"The tongue can bring death or life; those who love to talk will reap the consequences"* (Proverbs 18:21). It's no wonder that the New Testament writer, James, took special care to warn us about the power of the tongue.

> *Indeed, we all make many mistakes. For if we could control our tongues, we would be perfect and could also control ourselves in every other way. We can make a large horse go wherever we want by means of a small bit in its mouth. And a small rudder makes a huge ship turn wherever the pilot chooses to go, even though the winds are strong. In the same way, the tongue is a small thing that makes grand speeches. But a tiny spark can set a great forest on fire. And the tongue is a flame of fire. It is a whole world of wickedness, corrupting your entire body. It can set your whole life on fire, for it is set on fire by hell itself. People can tame all kinds of animals, birds, reptiles, and fish, but no one can tame the tongue. It is restless and evil, full of deadly poison* (James 3:2–8).

Perhaps this is why James dropped us a little piece of advice earlier in this same epistle: *"Understand this, my dear brothers and sisters: You must all be quick to listen, slow to speak, and slow to get angry"* (James 1:19). Think about it. This advice would actually make our lives so much less complicated. We don't need a psychological guru to tell us that guarding our tongues will improve our family life and work relationships.

And long before James wrote his pointed exhortation in the first century A.D., the Book of Ecclesiastes gave us some good instruction regarding the proper use of our tongues. *"The more words you speak, the less they mean. So what good are they?"* (Ecclesiastes 6:11)

We must discern what needs to be expressed and what might be better left unsaid. We need to acknowledge that, for the most part, we are not as smart as we think we are. Our words may not be as clever and witty as we envision them to be. And that morsel of gossip? Swallow it!

A few wise words can help the situation, but foolish spouting just exposes us as embarrassing big-mouths. *"Wise words bring approval, but fools are destroyed by their own words. Fools base their thoughts on foolish assumptions, so their conclusions will be wicked madness; they chatter on and on"* (Ecclesiastes 10:12–14).

The Teacher in this ancient book also reminded us that wise words are sometimes best delivered in a quiet peaceful manner where they can be heard with appreciation. *"Better to hear the quiet words of a wise person than the shouts of a foolish king"* (Ecclesiastes 9:17).

But timely words can also provide an uncomfortable yet necessary twinge that steers a wayward soul in the right direction. *"The words of the wise are like cattle prods— painful but helpful. Their collected sayings are like a nail-studded stick with which a shepherd drives the sheep"* (Ecclesiastes 12:11).

So, here is where the matter gets tricky. Some of us think we are reasonably bright; we believe that we have something to offer people by way of our wisdom and experience, especially to people younger than ourselves. How do we know when it's time to speak and when it's time to be quiet? How do we know how much to say if we are feeling led to say anything at all to someone who needs counsel?

To answer this, a glimpse at the life of Jesus might help. Sometimes Jesus spoke up quite aggressively, especially when it was time to challenge religious hypocrites defiling the truths of God. Sometimes he remained silent, especially when he was being falsely accused. Sometimes he preached sermons, but more often he just served people through miracles and other acts of love.

Now, we may not be turning water into wine at a friend's wedding, but we can serve that friend with our sacrificial efforts to ensure that the wedding is a success, as opposed to using our tongues to malign the bridesmaid dresses. We may not be healing a blind man, unable to see since birth, but we can give that blind man a meal or some shelter as opposed to talking about him behind his back, speculating who sinned to cause him to be born blind.

The greatest proportion of successful Christian service uses parts of the body other than the tongue. I suggest we follow Christ's example and focus on serving. Even the Gospel writers, like John, celebrated more what Jesus *did* in his ministry as opposed to what he *said* (John 21:25).

Consider again the story of Job that was referenced earlier in this chapter. If Job's friends had concentrated on serving their poor companion, rather than verbally denouncing him for supposedly harboring secret sin, there would have been a lot more healing and a lot less sinning. Listen to God's condemnation of the friends at the end of the story: *"I am angry with you…for you have not spoken accurately about me, as my servant Job has"* (Job 42:7). In fact, God called on Job to pray for them so they wouldn't be punished for their foolishness (Job 42:8).

In this case, the main problem for the friends wasn't excess words (for Job was more verbose than all his friends put together), the problem was that they did not speak rightly of God. They thought they were wise, but their theology was wrong—people suffer for many reasons, not just because they have sinned.

In Job's case, he never knew about the dialogue in Heaven between Satan and God. He was never informed of the fact that God vouched for him before the evil one. Now, throughout the account, Job said a lot of things about God that might have been correct, but this was not the time for human words; this was a time for submission to the Creator.

God did not congratulate Job for being intelligent. In fact, it was quite the opposite. The friends spoke wrongly; Job spoke too much.

After the humans were done talking in the story, God said to Job, *"Who is this that questions my wisdom with such ignorant words? Brace yourself like a man, because I have some questions for you, and you must answer them"* (Job 38:2–3). Or, as the Contemporary English Version says, *"Why do you talk so much when you know so little?"* (Job 38:2 CEV) God then proceeded to pronounce his supremacy over all Creation, and Job's corresponding ignorance on all matters divine. The blasting came in two waves.

But when the divine lectures were complete, Job did the right thing. He confessed the sins of his mouth, particularly his predisposition to intellectual presumption. Listen to the words of a man who came to understand how to use his mouth properly in the presence of a holy and omnipotent Creator: *"I am nothing—how could I ever find the answers? I will cover my mouth with my hand. I have said too much already. I have nothing more to say"* (Job 40:4–5). And again, *"You asked, 'Who is this that questions my wisdom with such ignorance?' It is I—and I was talking about things I knew nothing about, things far too wonderful for me...I take back everything I said, and I sit in dust and ashes to show my repentance"* (Job 42:3, 6).

We too can demonstrate this same response today. True glimpses of the glory of God drive us to repent, to recant, to take back the things we have said in ignorance or presumption, as well as the evil things we have allowed to flow from our tongues.

As usual, the message from God is plain and simple—whether it be in our relationship with the Lord or with our fellow man, God is looking for a few good words.

DISCUSSION QUESTIONS

1. What are some of the pitfalls of talking too much?

2. How does the Lord's Prayer exemplify brevity in talking with God?

3. What can Elijah's story on Mount Carmel teach us about offering a few good words to God?

4. What is the main idea of James' teaching on the tongue?

5. Summarize the Book of Ecclesiastes' instructions regarding the tongue.

6. Being mindful of God's warning to speak less, how do we know when it's time to speak up and when it's time to be quiet?

7. What was the problem with the words Job's friends offered him?

8. What was the problem with Job's words?

Chapter 5

"Sin—what a waste!"

*"Our desires make us sin,
and when sin is finished with us,
it leaves us dead."*

~ James 1:15 CEV

My wife and I often muse about how much time, effort, and money would be saved if we all sinned less.

Consider some of the time-consuming activities instigated by sin—cleaning up building façades damaged by vandalism, laboriously searching for the truth in every courtroom trial, nursing anorexic or bulimic children back to health, managing behavioral issues in a middle years classroom, waiting in Emergency to be treated for domestic dispute injuries, covering for co-workers faking sickness, serving jail sentences, picking up litter, and worrying for hours on end about every possible thing that might go wrong in life.

Think also about the money wasted by sin—the Twin Towers clean-up, forest fires started by arson, nuclear arms races, investment scams that clean out little old ladies' savings accounts, health care costs devoted to gluttony-related illnesses, penal system expenses, work productivity lost because of hangovers, and untold personal wealth consumed by pornography, gambling, and drug addictions.

At its most severe level, sin devours life through murder, rape, war, lynching, overdose, suicide, prostitution, and all forms of abuse—physical, sexual, substance, and psychological.

We are forced to put locks on everything we own and then spend fruitless hours looking for lost keys.

We are obliged to arrive two or three hours before an international flight because of the security measures required to deal with constant terrorist threats.

We are arguing with our spouses in the middle of the night when we should be sleeping because selfishness has transformed our marriages into complicated oratorical wrestling matches.

Sometimes, sin even breaks families totally apart, generating time-consuming activities of shuffling children between multiple households and sorting out complicated visitation arrangements during holiday seasons.

Unforgiveness can cause long-term friendships to disintegrate, depriving old buddies of the joy of future relationship, tossing them into a pit of bitterness.

Pastors who fall into sexual transgression shatter their reputations beyond repair and render useless what might have been an otherwise long and profitable ministry in the Kingdom of God.

And can we even begin to calculate the immeasurable sum total of the energy consumed by sinful habits practiced daily on this planet, whether it involve pride, greed, worry, pornography, soap operas, astrology, gossip, gluttony, substance abuse, criticism and anger, hatred and revenge, excessive TV-watching, dysfunctional control issues, compulsive lying, or obsessions ranging from compulsive cleanliness rituals to excessive body-building and make-up application? These activities eat up large portions of our day yet produce nothing good or useful for our families or our cultures.

I would even venture to guess that 90% of all police work consists of unproductive activity merely devoted to cleaning up sins' messes. As a civilization, we cannot devote the proper portion of our resources towards bettering society because we are forced to pay for the cost of bad behavior. Our money gets wasted on dealing with the ruination of sin.

What if more law enforcement dollars could be devoted towards vehicle safety issues and accident prevention programs? What if more health care revenue could be allocated to improve cancer screening techniques and to update expensive diagnostic equipment like MRI machines? What if a greater portion of the inordinately unbalanced business wealth in the world was shared with developing nations for clean water and disease prevention programs as opposed to remaining in North America where it is squandered on the superfluous cars and houses of the rich and famous?

Yes, sin and selfishness exact an enormous cost on our lives, our families, and our cultures. When we take the time to carefully examine the price tag, it is obvious that the waste is deplorable on every level.

Of course, this is not how we see it from a purely human perspective. Actually, we do not think about this topic much at all. When I Googled the phrase 'wastefulness of sin', I received a whopping forty sites (June 10, 2010). And even if we do think about the cost of sin, we tend to water things down—our sins become merely 'mistakes' or 'shortcomings'. We do not regularly take notice of the loss and destruction accompanying sin, especially when it is our own offenses in question. This is dangerous. God considers the travesty of sin to be a grave issue; we should concur.

Sometimes unwittingly and sometimes deliberately, we are lured by the *"fleeting pleasures of sin"* (Hebrews 11:25). Instead of recognizing our rebellion for what it is—a destructive revolt against God—we see our little dalliances as perks, well-deserved breaks from the stresses and strains of a hard day at work. We see our sinful samplings as mild and harmless sideshows to the daily grind. Or, perversely, we may even think of our little rabbit trails off the straight and narrow as acts of entitlement for our brilliant performances or our faithful service to God.

Regardless of how we see our sin, God sees it as a horrendous defilement of his plan. It violates his holy character and necessitated the murder of his innocent son, Jesus. We can't begin to comprehend how sin grieves the heart of our Creator. But we also blind ourselves to the tangible desecration caused by our offenses.

Sin trashes everything in God's Creation, like a gang of ignorant thugs senselessly tearing through a china shop with the sole purpose of causing as much destruction as possible. Our rebellion ravages all that could be used for good. It constantly works against God's plan for us to cultivate and govern the Earth properly (Genesis 1:28).

This reckless nature of sin was evident from the beginning. After the original couple sinned in the Garden of Eden, God warned them that life would now be more convoluted in their fallen state. Time and effort would now be wasted because of sin. Agriculture would be more difficult. Relationships would become more complicated. God said to Eve, *"You will desire to control your husband, but he will rule over you"* (Genesis 3:16). And to Adam,

> *Since you listened to your wife and ate from the tree whose fruit I commanded you not to eat, the ground is cursed because of you. All your life you will struggle to scratch a living from it. It will grow thorns and thistles for you, though you will eat of its grains. By the sweat of your brow will you have food to eat* (Genesis 3:17–19).

Woven throughout the biblical narrative is an ugly tapestry of devastation caused by sin. As soon as Adam and Eve realized their transgression, they began the long-standing human tradition of running from God. Instead of enjoying their daily fellowship with the Creator, where were they? Wasting time, hiding from him. The chronicle of resource dissipation had now officially begun. Consider some stories in the Book of Genesis.

The destruction of life and cultural development in The Flood was a result of horrendous sin and debauchery (Genesis 6:5–7). The resources used to construct the Tower of Babel were squandered because of immoral motives (Genesis 11:1–9). Abraham had to waste his time and effort rescuing Lot from captivity, all because his nephew was kidnapped from a sinful city where he did not belong in the first place (Genesis 14). Laban's lies ended up wasting twenty years of Jacob's life in the simple process of securing a wife (Genesis 31:36–42). Shechem's rape of Dinah triggered a chain of events that led to the destruction and looting of an entire city and the murder of its male population (Genesis 34). The treachery of Joseph's brothers and the deception of Potiphar's wife consumed the prime years of this young man's life and exhausted the emotions of a troubled father who needlessly grieved his son's 'death' for over twenty years (Genesis 37:2 cf. 41:46). And these are but a few examples from just the first book of the Bible.

As a nation, Israel wasted forty years in the wilderness because of their sinful disbelief in God. What if we were to examine the repetitive and useless cycle of sin recorded in the Book of Judges or the wastefulness of the evil monarchs who ruled over the split kingdoms of Israel and Judah? And, of course, there is the all-time New Testament classic illustration of squander—the Prodigal Son.

The blueprint seems quite consistent. Sin devours. Consider Psalm 106:13–15. When the Israelites *"quickly forgot His works...[and]...did not wait for His counsel, but craved intensely in the wilderness, and tempted God in the desert...[the Almighty]...gave them their request, but sent a wasting disease among them"* (Psalm 106:13–15 NASB).

When we strive for what we want instead of what God wants for us, there is a consequence that involves some form of harmful consumption. The New Testament writer James explains it this way: *"Temptation comes from our own desires, which entice us and drag us away. These desires give birth to sinful actions. And when sin is allowed to grow, it gives birth to death"* (James 1:14–15). Death is the ultimate consumer of assets and resources.

Probably one of the strongest explanations of the waste of sin is recorded in Deuteronomy 28. This chapter outlined two options for God's chosen people—blessings for obeying the Lord, and curses for disobedience. The blessings span fourteen verses, but the curses, fifty-four. And the curses comprise a vast array of the depleting effects of sin, including physical and mental health issues, confusion, destruction, defeat, lack of basic necessities, deterioration of relationship, asset deprivation, environmental suffering, enslavement, self-consumption, loss of dignity, lack of productivity and prosperity, loss of property, deprivation of rest, escalation of fear, a return to sinful habits, and even oppression for future offspring (Deuteronomy 28:15–68).

Now, the church operates under a different administration than Israel experienced in fifteenth century B.C., but the principle inherent in this passage seems to be part of God's thinking throughout all time. God wants us to be holy and productive. The spiritual forces of darkness want us to be confused and unproductive. Satan enjoys making God's creatures useless. He loves to persuade us to waste our lives and our gifts.

Consider the obvious examples in the New Testament where demons were involved in controlling or influencing humans. The results were never fruitful. Demon-possessed people lost their independence (Luke 4:33–35), their youth (Mark 9:21), their sanity (Luke 8:35), their self-control (Matthew 8:28), their physical health (Luke 13:11), their sight (Matthew 12:22), their hearing (Mark 9:25), their speech (Luke 11:14), and even their clothes (Luke 8:27). Demons instigated epilepsy (Matthew 17:14–18), convinced people to self-mutilate (Mark 5:5), imparted destructive super-human strength (Mark 5:4), caused a farmer's entire herd of swine to commit suicide (Mark 5:13), and victimized a young girl by enslaving her to unscrupulous profiteers (Acts 16:16–18). You see, it's all about loss and desecration. It's always about rendering a life useless, spent, and impotent.

One of the all-time greatest examples in more recent history of personal waste encouraged by demonic oppression has to be the story of the Winchester House in San Jose, California. In 2004, I visited this famous house and saw the uncanny construction for myself. The story is remarkable and tragic.

In 1862, Sarah Pardee married William Wirt Winchester, just as he was beginning to reel in huge profits from his newly improved Winchester Repeater. Throughout the Civil War and beyond, Winchester amassed a personal fortune from government contracts as well as from the private sales of his successful rifle.

Sadly though, along with their growing riches, the Winchesters experienced heart-wrenching tragedies. In 1866, their only child died nine days after birth, sending Sarah into a decade of depression. Then, in 1881, William himself passed away from tuberculosis. The widowed Sarah was left with a broken heart and more money than she knew what to do with—$20 million and 48.9% ownership of a company that generated her a non-taxable income of $1000 per day. Today, that would be the equivalent of over $20 000 a day.[8]

In the midst of her sorrow, Mrs. Winchester sought comfort in the counsel of a medium. The spiritualist told Sarah that she was cursed because of the terrible weapon created by her husband. Supposedly, the spirits of thousands of victims shot by Winchester rifles had now assembled to seek their revenge on Sarah, the lone surviving member of the family.

The medium said Sarah's husband would guide her westward and would direct her to purchase the appropriate home which she was to renovate according to the spirits' instructions. As long as she kept building, she was told, she would live. If she stopped, she would die.[9]

In 1884, she arrived in the Santa Clara Valley and purchased a six-room home under construction on a 162–acre

[8] http://en.wikipedia.org/wiki/Winchester_Mystery_House
[9] http://www.prairieghosts.com/winchester.html

parcel of land. She threw away the original house plans and started down a road of colossal waste and confusion. She employed dozens of local carpenters to work on the project, twenty-four hours a day, seven days a week.

For thirty-eight years, they built, demolished, rebuilt, and added on to the house until it grew into a monstrosity of perplexing proportion and design. At its peak, it boasted about 160 rooms (impossible to count exactly), seven stories, three elevators, six kitchens, forty staircases, forty bedrooms, forty-seven fireplaces, fifty-two skylights, 950 doors, and 10 000 window panes.[10]

Every morning she would receive instructions from the spirits for the day's construction. She would pass on these chaotic directions to her foremen who attempted to carry out her peculiar plans. Every day, for the rest of her life, Sarah devoted all her energy and passion into the house, draining nearly every penny of her massive fortune.

Even after the great San Francisco earthquake of 1906 reduced the structure from seven stories to four, and left much of the house in ruins, Sarah pressed on. She even proceeded with a clever maneuver that involved boarding up thirty damaged rooms in the front of the house to prevent the work from ever being truly completed, thus preserving her protection from the malevolent spirits—who, again, would kill her if she stopped building.

When I visited the house myself, I could see the nonsense that these demons had dragged this poor woman through for almost four decades. There is no logical layout to the mansion. It's just plain stupid. There are staircases that lead to nowhere, useless chimneys all over the place, doors that open to steep drops to the lawn below, rooms within rooms, upside down stair posts, closet doors in front of blank walls, washrooms with glass doors, and a winding staircase of forty-two steps, each two inches high. The house is an insane maze. After her

---

[10] http://www.winchestermysteryhouse.com/facts.html

death, it took workmen more than six weeks to get the furniture out of what looks more like a labyrinth than a residential dwelling. Even today, visitors need guides to avoid getting lost within the mansion.

What a mammoth waste of time. What a colossal consumption of one of the world's largest fortunes in its day. What an enormous emaciation of a life. But as I said, that's what sin does—it wastes. And that's what demons do—create in us not necessarily a hatred for God, but an apathy and forgetfulness towards him, causing us to get lost in worlds of meaningless misuse.

Instead of her sinful obsession with nonsensical self-preservation, consider the good this woman could have done with her robust inheritance. Sarah Winchester could have devoted her time and money towards acts of social reform. She could have adopted orphans or built homes for widows less fortunate than herself. She could have created schools for children on the streets or foundations that supported the homeless and destitute in her community.

Any of these acts would have taught her that, truly, *"it is more blessed to give than to receive"* (Acts 20:35). But instead, Sarah knew only obsession and fear. Sin sucked the life out of her and all her potential. This story is particularly sad when we consider her as a youngster in New Haven, Connecticut. History tells us that

> … as she reached maturity, she became the belle of the city. She was well-received at all social events, thanks to her musical skills, her fluency in various foreign languages and her sparkling charm. Her beauty was also well-known by the young men about town, despite her diminutive size. Although she was petite and stood only four feet, ten inches, she made up for this in personality and loveliness.[11]

---

[11] Cited June 10, 2010 http://www.prairieghosts.com/winchester.html

In 1922, shortly after her daily conference session with the spirits in the séance room, Sarah died at the age of 83, a broken and fragile remnant of what she might have been.

Perhaps our stories are not as dramatic as Sarah Winchester's, but we would be wise to examine ourselves to see where we have allowed sin and selfishness to penetrate our lives to the point of obvious consumption. We need to ponder what we are accomplishing with the window of opportunity God has given us to serve him. Are our time, money, love, attention, care, and compassion being invested into our families, friends, widows, orphans, and the needy—into the Kingdom of God? Or are they being frittered away by sinful habits?

This is a call for repentance, a plea to tear out some faulty human thinking. When we have a change of mind about our sin, and desire to seek God's forgiveness, we need to comprehend the travesty of sin in all its fullness. Yes, in light of God's holiness, our sin is ugly; unrepented sin separates us from him. But there is more—we also need to confess the wastefulness of our sin. We need to cry out to God for forgiveness—forgiveness for squandering on ourselves the gifts he has given us for his Kingdom and for his glory.

We need to repent of the wastefulness of our sin. Perhaps as we do this with more understanding, the lure of future sin might seem a little less attractive.

DISCUSSION QUESTIONS

1. What are some of the most wasteful consequences of sin?

2. What destructive behaviors did evil spirits instigate in the New Testament accounts of demon possession?

3. What are some of the mind games we play to minimize the seriousness of our sinful behaviour?

4. Like Adam and Eve, what are some of the ways we waste our time 'hiding from God'?

5. What does Deuteronomy 28 teach us about the depleting effects of sin?

6. What does the story of Sarah Winchester tell us about the motive of demons?

7. What does it mean to comprehend the travesty of sin in all its fullness?

8. Can you identify a period in your life where sin consumed you?

Chapter 6

"I am tolerant of intolerance."

"Don't just pretend to love others. Really love them.
Hate what is wrong. Hold tightly to what is good.
Love each other with genuine affection
and take delight in honoring each other."

~ Romans 12:9–10

In today's society, it seems that one of the most heinous labels that can be assigned to a person is the tag of intolerance. Gluttony, selfishness, cowardice—yes, these are bad behaviors—but the hideous and grotesque monster lurking amongst us, we are told, is the person who is intolerant, especially the religious kind.

Human thinking at this point in history has arrived at a rather perplexing paradigm regarding personal discernment. Historians may look back at this period in Western philosophy as a time when it was illegal, or certainly ill-advised, to have an opinion on moral matters.

The enlightened uberthinker of the twenty-first century is touted as the individual who loves everyone indiscriminately, celebrates all possible forms of diversity, and accepts all behaviour, no matter how bizarre. We are told that we have no right to cast judgment upon others because objective truth is non-existent. Any person who ventures to express a concern about a particular lifestyle or behavioral practice risks being brutally attacked by the guardians of the great deity of secular pluralism.

I must admit—I don't like to be branded as blatantly intolerant. The term has come to be associated with bigotry, prejudice, fanaticism, and small-minded thinking. Naturally, I don't want to be perceived as a pea-brained idiot who goes around judging, cursing, or harming people I don't even know.

But I also want to be free to think, to reason critically, and to form opinions based on my search for truth. And so should you. In the past, liberal-minded secularists were offended by the moralistic censorship of the religious right (probably more turned off by their style than their message); but now we have a censorship of a different kind. Whenever someone on a public platform utters a conservative or Christian social commentary on contemporary mores, he or she is branded an intolerant pig.

This is shamefully unfair. Consider the matter of abortion, for example. Most pro-lifers are not depraved and insecure boors who want to impose their morality on others just because they have nothing better to do until their next Sunday school class. No. Many pro-lifers are genuinely concerned about the pregnant mother. They fear that she will regret her decision down the road and will never be able to reverse the guilt. They question whether personal comfort and convenience should take precedence over the sanctity of life. They are troubled that one mistake might become two. And they're concerned about the health risks that may accompany such a dramatic 'procedure' (a euphemism for ripping a life out of a womb, because it is easier to tolerate euphemisms than real words). The motives of moral absolutists may be more complex than liberal critics are willing to concede.

Agreed, pure hateful intolerance is dreadful. There has been no shortage of nonsense done in the name of religion over the centuries. Christianity's treatment of the Jews throughout history has been horrendous. The Inquisition's handling of non-Catholics in the 16th century is grievously sad. Religious intolerance killed 35% of Germany's population in the 17th century during the Thirty Years War as Catholics and

Protestants slaughtered each other mercilessly.[12] And the witch hunts of the 16th and 17th centuries resulted in the abhorrent treatment of hundreds of thousands of women, most of whom were innocent of any criminal or immoral activity.[13]

But religious folk do not have the market cornered on intolerance. There have been plenty of acts of murderous fanaticism that had little to do with religious creed. The blatantly racist whites of the American South committed unspeakable crimes against other humans, solely because their parents taught them to hate people with a different level of melanin in their skin. The late 20th century conflict between the Hutus and Tutsis, though possessing the same basic level of melanin, resulted in the greatest genocide of our generation. Even class conflicts have brought about horrendous suffering for tens of millions—Stalin's annihilation of the kulaks in the inter-war years exemplifies paranoid insecure intolerance at its worst.

Fanatical commitment to brutalizing other people with different ideas or nose sizes is appalling, regardless of its philosophical origin. All brands of humans can be hatefully and destructively intolerant. In our fallen state, we are capable of very injurious conduct towards our brothers and sisters. Whether through brainwashing or simple selfishness, any action that does not respect our fellow human as a divine image-bearer is wrong, and should cease.

But secular human thinking has created a great deal of confusion regarding the idea of tolerance. Wholesale tolerance is based on the premise that there are no moral absolutes. Post-modern thinkers consider themselves to have progressed beyond the condemning and restrictive posture of past generations. They deem themselves to be the liberators of free-thinkers who used to be squashed or even persecuted for

---

[12] Cited June 10, 2010 http://users.erols.com/mwhite28/
warstat0.htm#European
[13] Cited June 10, 2010 http://en.wikipedia.org/wiki/Witch-hunt

their differences of opinion and lifestyle. This current view of tolerance and intolerance is faulty on several levels.

Inconsistencies abound.

If tolerance truly is the highest virtue, then all positions and opinions should receive fair and equal treatment; all should be free from harassment or ridicule. But in reality, post-modern tolerance appears to be tolerant of all religions except Christianity. Late-night talk show hosts can mock out Christian principles or public figures, much to the delight of applauding audiences. What would happen if those same TV personalities mocked out Buddhism or Hinduism? Their careers could be over in a heartbeat. True tolerance should tolerate all views, not just those on the liberal agenda.

Secondly, indiscriminate tolerance is just pure nonsense from a logical standpoint. How can absolutely everything be right? There are obvious limits to tolerance. Some actions should not be accepted or even endured because of the deliberate harm they inflict on humanity. Who besides the psychologically disturbed or the criminally insane would think Jeffrey Dahmer's actions are tolerable? There is no room at the discussion table for serial murder and cannibalism.

Other contenders for general exclusion might include bestiality, child pornography, female circumcision, crystal meth trafficking, sex slavery, genocide, and NAMBLA, just to name a few. NAMBLA (North American Man Boy Love Association) has a very troubling main objective—the legal abolishment of age restraint regarding sexual involvement. To put it bluntly, they want to have sex with little boys and not go to jail. There should be no forum for people who want to lower the age of sexual consent to the vicinity of potty-training.

Thirdly, some individuals who claim to be universally and compassionately open-minded may be more tolerant in word than in deed. An ultra-liberal who proudly pronounces her support of sexual liberation may even be willing to tolerate the philosophies and political lobbying of NAMBLA. But how would that same mother feel if several of their members moved in next door and began to leer over the fence at her four-year-old twin boys playing in the backyard?

The notion of tolerance can be quite paradoxical. Is it necessary to be a tolerant person? If that means loving all people, yes! If that means being apathetic, no! Can odious intolerance hurt people? Of course! But are there times when one needs to stand against something that seems to be wrong? Absolutely! Tolerance plays a key role in the life of a Christian and in any civilized culture. But tolerance was never meant to be the driver of the bus. From God's perspective, that role is to be played by love. And love is not just blanket tolerance—more on that later.

The concept of tolerance is not as black and white as secular humanists make it out to be. Like I said before, it's not just the secular who are tolerant and the religious who are intolerant. Consider the current origin of life debate. Compared to the Intelligent Design group, there appears to be far more intolerance in the evolutionary science camp who insist on a closed system, disallowing the possibility of divine intervention in the Universe.

As well, people cannot be lumped into two simple laundry piles of lights and darks—tolerant and intolerant. Different situations call for different responses.

As a father raising young children, I needed to discern which of their behaviors I would tolerate and those I would not. Sometimes I put up with my child's immaturity, knowing that my patience would help fertilize a healthier plant in the future. On other occasions, my children learned that I was not going to stand for certain behaviors. Some things could not be passed off as childish, or viewed as alternative options. No, I would address the action as unacceptable, clearly communicating what needed to change. But as I acted out my 'intolerance' of their improper behavior, I did it out of love, trying not to be ignorant or insensitive to their feelings or damaging to their psyche.

Even Jesus moved between expressions of tolerance and intolerance in his earthly ministry. With the woman caught in adultery, Jesus was charitable with her because he saw a broken and repentant heart that was willing to move forward into a new life (John 8:1–11). But with the Pharisees, Jesus came across as quite intolerant, unwilling to put up with their wicked ways and wrong thinking. He called them blind fools, snakes, and hypocrites (Matthew 23). Because of the deception on their tongues and the hardness of their hearts, Jesus let them have it. It grieved the Lord that these religious leaders were hurting so many people with their personal sins and their inconsistent theology.

So, it's not as straightforward as we want it to be. And certain key words are gaining a lot of power in the debate. Inclusion and harmony have emerged as the new Twin Towers rising high on the horizon of our post-modern world. There exists this simplistic notion that the diversity of a pluralistic society produces its best melodious harmonies when all its parts are included and allowed to play. The assumption is that the music will be of poorer quality when certain instruments are prohibited from participating.

In the non-metaphoric realm of music, such a notion is true. Different notes coming together form something more interesting and more beautiful than a single note. But in our sinfully saturated society, are we correct to assume that all notes should be sung? Every single political view? Every cult? Every fringe organization? Again, NAMBLA? Is there no test?

Even from a common sense perspective, what is the basis for the belief that all positions should be equally valued, especially when we consider the criminal, the insane, the terrorist, the bi-sexual? Sorry about my pet peeve—I have trouble mustering sympathy for a cause consisting of people who think they need to have sex with everybody. Don't we need to discriminate and choose what seems right, good, and decent—what truly moves us towards a 'do no harm' philosophy?

When we speak of the glories of inclusion and harmony, some of it makes perfect sense. We indeed declare the glory of God and preserve the dignity of his Creation when we embrace and celebrate people of varying race, ethnicity, gender, class, language, age, and ability. But, again, we need to discern.

To begin to sort out much of our muddled human thinking on tolerance, we need to take a closer look at the original meaning of this word that has come to be the center of so much debate.

The word tolerance comes from the Latin *tolerantia*, meaning to bear or endure, in the sense of enduring a burden.[14] At its root meaning, the term implies putting up with someone or something. For example, we talk about how much pain a person can tolerate.

In light of this, tolerance makes sense solely in a moral context. The term only has meaning when there is deep passion or concern on the part of the players in the story. You need to feel strongly about your position before you can claim to be tolerant of someone else's.

Only where there is right and wrong can there be individuals who believe they are right, but bear or endure others who appear to be wrong. To tolerate someone else's opinion means that, though I feel strongly about my position and believe it to be right, I will put up with you and your position. I disagree with you, but I will not be a jerk towards you.

In a world of moral relativism, there can be no true tolerance since there is no objective point from which to judge. True tolerance means that, even though you think your opponent is wrong (a moral judgment), you graciously choose to bear the burden of his difference. If everything and everybody is right, what is there to tolerate?

---

[14] Cited on April 19, 2009 http://dictionary.reference.com/browse/tolerance

We have been using the word tolerance quite freely since Voltaire and the Age of Enlightenment, but post-modern secularists have employed it to produce a smoke screen that has fooled many people as to what is really going on. I think we've been duped. Contrary to popular opinion, we don't have universal tolerance—we have universal apathy. In the absence of a moral code and solid family foundations, we have lost our way in a haze of hedonism. The act of stimulating our senses has been elevated over the value of life. Many people proudly wear the blazer of total tolerance, but truth be told, they really don't care about anything but themselves.

Blind and arbitrary tolerance is not necessarily a love for all mankind; it may be a general disdain for humanity. It may represent an abandonment of what common sense tells us is good. It may be a concession that hope is lost, a disbelief in a better future. What a pitiful stance! If I see my friend sleeping with a different woman every weekend, why would I not confront him? Why would I remain apathetic to the destruction coming his way?

So then, another concept seems to be coming to light— there appears to be both good and bad tolerance, as well as good and bad intolerance. Most Germans in the 1930's did not know where their horrendous tale was about to take them; but still, most Germans were wrongfully tolerant of Hitler's ill-treatment of the Jews, long before the Holocaust was in full fruition. To their shame, they, as well as most of the West, bore the burden of seeing fellow humans lose their civil rights, but failed to make a concerted effort to stop it, permitting it to spin out of control. So, Hitler was wrongfully intolerant and full of hatred, while most of his patriotic followers were wrongfully tolerant and full of indifference. Either way, humanity suffered atrociously.

Granted, the secular world seems to have figured out this concept of good and bad tolerance/intolerance in some areas. For example, a group of friends may organize an intervention because one in their midst is hurting herself by a harmful habit; this friend needs her behaviors to be *not* tolerated. Such positive peer pressure is intended to drive out the negative behavior which has become part of her habitual lifestyle. The intolerance of the friends is helpful in that it demonstrates a high level of love for the fallen comrade.

Another example of helpful intolerance would be our change in attitude towards the use of tobacco. In North America, smoking is no longer tolerated in most public places because it is so obvious that it harms other people. This cultural shift does not reflect a hate for smokers, but an act of common sense for the good of all.

Also quite common in our alcohol-laden culture is the recitation, "Friends don't let friends drive drunk." Why? Because when we tolerate inebriated drivers, people get hurt. Duh! Why would we sit back and just tolerate behavior that hurts the ones we love and care about?

Yes, tolerance can be an act of love, but it can also be an act of apathy. And intolerance can be an act of love or an act of hatred and ignorance. It boils down to the motive and character of the dispenser. Love is the universal good— sometimes that love is played out through responses of tolerance, and sometimes it is displayed through actions of intolerance. We tolerate because we love, but sometimes we don't tolerate because we love. As I alluded to earlier, this is the essence of good parenting.

To be more specific, good tolerance needs to be seen as a patient and caring treatment of the person possessing the different view, not an acceptance of their position or behavior. We are called to be tolerant of people, but not necessarily their practices if we are convinced that their actions are wrong or detrimental.

Now, you may be asking yourself, where is God in all of this?

I have purposefully limited the voice of the Creator in our discussion so far because he can be a little distracting. Why? Because he's such an easy target. Regularly, humans

condemn God the Father as the ultimate intolerant
personality. There is this perverted view of God as an all-
powerful deity who wants only to say "No!" to everyone's
fun. He is branded as the definitive downer who sucks the
life out of every party and condemns all that represents free-
thinking and liberation. This stunted view of our loving God
is disgraceful but popular.

Obviously, God must deal with man's unrepentant
behavior and humanistic approach to life. He hates sin. God,
in his holiness, is pressed by his very nature to respond
harshly to willful transgression. The whole purpose of God's
plan is the restoration of all Creation (Acts 3:21); naturally
this involves the eradication of sin (Romans 5:12–19).

In ancient times, God flooded the Earth to punish the
wickedness that he could no longer tolerate (Genesis 6:11–13).
On occasion, he judged people for putting up with evil, rather
than addressing it. Eli was scolded for tolerating the vile acts
of his two sons in their role as priests; their iniquity brought
about their premature deaths (I Samuel 3:12–13). The Apostle
Paul rebuked the members of the Corinthian church because
they were arrogantly tolerating a member in their midst who
was sleeping with his stepmother (1 Corinthians 5:1–13). Even
Jesus on the cross experienced the abandonment of the Father
because a holy God could not look upon his beloved son
bearing our sins (Matthew 27:46).

And at the final judgment, God's holiness will condemn
sinners to eternal damnation because of their evil deeds
(Revelation 20:12–13) and their rejection of salvation in
Christ (I John 5:11–12). We must not be silly. Whoever
creates the Universe gets to make the rules. God cannot
tolerate sin. But he never ceases from having compassion for
the sinner in the process.

While we live out our journeys on this Earth, God
actually appears to be quite tolerant of his faltering creatures.
He bears the burden of our willful disobedience. Though our
sin grieves him, he is very patient with humanity. In fact, he is

so kind and long-suffering with sinners, onlookers think evil may never be punished (2 Peter 3:3–7). But God assures us that the delay in Christ's return is not because he is merely tolerating sin; he is giving people more time to repent and escape destruction (2 Peter 3:8–9).

Old truth is still true—God loves the sinner but hates the sin. Perhaps calling God tolerant is confusing, but consider the facts. God will wait and watch his Creation stubbornly go its own way over a prolonged period of time. He longs for repentance and a change of heart. He yearns for fellowship with his children. That is why he offered up Jesus as a sacrifice for sin. But while he continues to pour out his love for us, he never stops despising the sin in our lives that will destroy us.

Is God tolerant? He is patient, that's for sure. He puts up with me, and there are almost seven billion of us rebels on this little ball of rock. If God wasn't tolerant, we'd all be dead in an instant.

In all fairness, I acknowledge that people who take up the torch of tolerance as a special cause in their lives are committed to many good principles. They believe society becomes richer with greater diversity. I agree. They believe people should not suffer persecution for being different than the norms of their society. Again, I agree. Hatred-based intolerance is criminal and loathsome. It has initiated untold human anguish.

To make progress in the dialogue, we need to respect each other. We need to be patient and kind, and we need to listen. But we also need a new approach. The old one has not worked.

Instead of the fruitless debate of tolerance vs. intolerance, let's put our issues on continuums where we can discuss them more truthfully. These continuums would display various options for where we might each draw our own lines of intolerance. It's not as if some people are tolerant and others are intolerant. Everyone is intolerant at some point.

Let me illustrate. Consider the topic of sexual practice. Its continuum might look like this:

←——————————————————————————————————→

NAMBLA Bestiality Bisexual Homosexual Heterosexual Heterosexual Abstinence
                                           free for all   in marriage

Don't get hung up on the exact order; this is just an idea. Consider how you might re-arrange the items on the line and where you personally would draw your own line of intolerance. Could you talk about your position with someone else and not hate them at the end of the conversation? That's a start.

Consider another continuum. How about drug use?

←——————————————————————————————————→

Meth Heroin Cocaine Ecstasy Marijuana Nicotine Alcohol Prescription Caffeine
                                                               Drugs

Respectful dialogue stems from recognizing that we all draw our lines of intolerance at different spots on the continuum. The debate should not be over tolerance vs. intolerance, but rather where to draw the line and why? As these conversations happen in peaceful and intelligent environments, the love of Christians has a chance to impact open hearts and minds.

So then, what is required of those who want to think like God and follow Jesus? Obviously, a believer is exhorted to differentiate between right and wrong. The writer of Hebrews refers to mature believers as those who, by practicing the righteous teachings of God's Word, *"have trained themselves to distinguish good from evil"* (Hebrews 5:14 NIV).

But this discernment must always be done in the context of love. Listen to the Apostle Paul in Romans 12:9–10: *"Don't just pretend to love others. Really love them. Hate what is wrong. Hold tightly to what is good. Love each other with genuine affection and take delight in honoring each other."* Nestled in the middle of this love sandwich is the meat of discernment. Genuinely love people in your world and deal with the evil in your own life. Embrace what is good so that your love and godly character may inspire others to do the same. We are not to make unbelievers feel hated because they are living apart from God's standards. The main idea is love.

Later in this same passage, Paul goes on to explain more fully what this love looks like:

> *Live in harmony with each other. Don't be too proud to enjoy the company of ordinary people. And don't think you know it all! Never pay back evil with more evil. Do things in such a way that everyone can see you are honorable. Do all that you can to live in peace with everyone. Dear friends, never take revenge. Leave that to the righteous anger of God. For the Scriptures say, "I will take revenge; I will pay them back," says the Lord* (Romans 12:16–19).

Notice the key concepts—live in harmony and peace with people, be humble, be honorable, don't take up the role of God's enforcer. Reading this, I would conclude that we should rarely blow anything up. Concern for issues (e.g. abortion) should always be accompanied by solutions to the problems (i.e. helping address the challenges faced by teenage girls with ill-timed pregnancies). Maybe that is what Paul meant when he said, *"Don't let evil conquer you, but conquer evil by doing good"* (Romans 12:21).

As we conclude this lengthy discussion, let's tie it all together by examining the life of Paul, before *and* after he was transformed by the saving blood of Jesus Christ.

In his pre-conversion days, the Apostle Paul was consumed with human thinking. As a zealous Jewish Pharisee, he was completely intolerant of Christianity. He mistakenly took it upon himself to mete out God's judgment on these 'heretics'. He persecuted the Christians by dragging them off to prison, forcing them to curse Jesus, and even having them killed. In his own words, *"I was so violently opposed to them that I even chased them down in foreign cities"* (Acts 26:11).

He was like an obsessed madman, almost out of control with his rage against these people who were different than him. This is bad intolerance.

But Paul also practiced bad tolerance before he was saved. As a hard-core Pharisee, he put up with a lot of hypocritical behavior within his religious organization. I don't imagine the sect in Paul's day was any more pristine than when Jesus described it a few years earlier, just before his crucifixion (Matthew 23). It's reasonable to assume that Paul would have looked the other way many times when his brothers failed to practice true righteousness, pretending to be holy by keeping the miniscule details of the law while neglecting *"justice, mercy and faith...the more important things"* (Matthew 23:23). This is bad tolerance.

But notice the change after his conversion. As a man injected with the Holy Spirit, forgiven by God, trained by hardship and the love of Christ, we see a new man—a man thinking more like God. And what do we notice? Paul now practiced both a tolerance and intolerance that was good and healthy.

A saved and regenerated Paul was now tolerant of abuse, abandonment, and betrayal by friends. Instead of hatred and violence for those who thought differently than him, Paul poured out his entire life to love, plead, and exhort people into the Kingdom of God. Instead of attacking those who disagreed with him, he wept for them (Acts 20:19, 31). Instead of putting his opponents to death, he himself was willing to endure incredible suffering for the name of Christ (Acts 21:13). In Christ, Paul was a new man. He was tolerant. He was kind. He was full of a supernatural love.

But he was also aware that God demands holiness of his people. So at appropriate moments, Paul also demonstrated a healthy intolerance towards sin that was harming those people he loved. For instance, when he wrote his first letter to the Corinthian church, he had to chastise them for a number of poor behaviors, the worst of which was the fact, as was

mentioned earlier, that one of their members was having sex
with his stepmom (1 Corinthians 5:1–11). Rightly so, Paul
spoke against this. He said to his fellow believers, *"You must
not simply look the other way and hope it goes away on its
own. Bring it out in the open and deal with it in the authority
of Jesus our Master"* (1 Corinthians 5:3 MSG).

But if you carefully read all of 1 Corinthians, you will
notice that Paul's intolerance is largely directed at the
immorality *within* the church. Those who claim to be
followers of Christ are subject to such judgments. Those
outside the church are just to be loved. Paul tells the believers,
*"It isn't my responsibility to judge outsiders, but it certainly is
your responsibility to judge those inside the church who are
sinning. God will judge those on the outside"* (1 Corinthians
5:12–13).

In all that has been said on this topic, perhaps Paul's
thoughts here represent the most useful and simple
summary—let's become a little more loving and tolerant of
other people outside the church, and a little more intolerant of
the wrongdoing within the church, especially the sin and
hypocrisy that lingers in our own lives. These could be some
simple first steps towards thinking like God on this matter.

DISCUSSION QUESTIONS

1. What is the current worldly perspective on tolerance and intolerance?

2. Give examples of religious and non-religious intolerance in the past.

3. How are post-modern thinkers sometimes inconsistent in their wholesale tolerance?

4. Are there some behaviors that even pagans would consider intolerable?

5. What is the original meaning of the word tolerance and how does that impact our understanding of the topic?

6. What role do the concepts of inclusion and harmony play in this discussion?

7. How might behavioral continuums help in the discussion of moral matters?

8. How does the life of Paul exemplify both good and bad tolerance and intolerance?

Chapter 7

"I love to find lost things."

*"The Son of Man came to seek and save
those who are lost."*

~ Luke 19:10

When I was eight years old, I got lost in Stanley Park in the city of Vancouver. For over an hour, I wandered around this 1000–acre woodland, wondering if I would ever see my family again. For my parents, it was one of the longest hours of their lives.

Being lost is a horrible feeling. A sense of panic overwhelms your soul. You feel frantic, speculating whether or not you'll ever be found, or find your way out. Most of us have experienced the anxiety of being lost or participated in the frenzied search for a missing child.

Entertainment executives know the attraction of storylines involving lost people. From the silliness of *Gilligan's Island* to the angst of Tom Hank's *Castaway* to the alluring emotions of ABC's critically acclaimed and successful serial drama of the 2000's, we are captivated by accounts of people who suddenly find themselves lost.

Today, satellite technology has eliminated some of the likelihood of getting lost. Whether at sea, up on a mountain, or hiking in the middle of the boonies, GPS tracking devices allow us to pinpoint our location with amazing accuracy. Such technology has given us an exaggerated sense of confidence in knowing where we are.

Although we may be able to find our way out of a forest with ease or retrace the exact spot where the fish were biting so furiously yesterday, mankind is still far more lost than we realize.

The general human consensus is that we are doing very well. Here's a news flash—no, we're not. Even though secular humanists perceive us to be evolving into a higher and higher form of intelligent life, in some ways we're getting dumber. We're lost and we don't even know it.

When we maneuver independently of God's direction for our lives, we are like clueless tourists traveling in a foreign country with no knowledge of the language. We're following our gut instincts, but unknowingly going in the wrong direction. Without Christ, we are spiritually *"lost in darkness"* (Romans 2:19), even if we don't recognize it. And this kind of lost is not like losing a game where we get another chance to be successful; the lostness of a human soul has grave and eternal consequences.

The Scriptures are adamant about portraying willful humans apart from God as lost sheep. Isaiah wrote: *"All of us, like sheep, have strayed away. We have left God's paths to follow our own"* (Isaiah 53:6). Speaking through Jeremiah, God affirmed this fact: *"My people have been lost sheep. Their shepherds have led them astray and turned them loose in the mountains. They have lost their way and can't remember how to get back to the sheepfold"* (Jeremiah 50:6). As a matter of personal confession, the Psalmist agreed: *"I have wandered away like a lost sheep: come and find me"* (Psalm 119:176).

In his ministry, Jesus perceived the general masses in much the same way. *"When he saw the crowds, he had compassion on them because they were confused and helpless, like sheep without a shepherd"* (Matthew 9:36). He referred to his fellow countrymen in need of salvation as *"the lost sheep of the house of Israel"* (Matthew 15:24 NASB) and called himself *"the Good Shepherd"* (John 10:11).

Fortunately, the good news is clear. God is very interested in finding those who are lost, and restoring them to their intended position of security and blessing. God does not want anyone to perish (Matthew 18:10–14). He does not leave us to guess his thoughts on this matter. The concept of *the lost* is very prevalent in his mind. In fact, God loves to find the lost. He is deeply committed to the project.

On the contrary, the average person spends very little time thinking about the lostness of humanity. Like any other regular guy, I experience sadness and frustration over lost keys, dogs, and contacts. But as a believer, what is my attitude towards those in this world who are spiritually lost? And what am I prepared to sacrifice to aid their rescue?

Because we are brainwashed by a worldly system run by a devil totally bent on deceiving us, we have a hard time believing that we are truly lost in our natural state. If life is clipping along fairly well for us, we may believe we have it all together. We don't feel lost.

Sometimes it takes utter despair or an experience of total brokenness to make us aware of our true position outside of God's Kingdom, to help us see that we need a Savior. It took the Prodigal Son a long time to realize that he was lost. But when he finally did, he knew what to do about it—run home to his father. In contrast to the son's eureka moment, most of the world continues to soldier on, totally oblivious to the reality of their spiritual lostness.

There is a measure of dullness here. Certainly, sheep can be dumb animals; so when God equates mankind with wooly quadrupeds, he is saying something very harsh but true about me. Left to my own devices, I will wander off to do stupid and harmful things. But God sent his son to find me and every other lost little lamb that is willing to acknowledge their need for a Savior. I know that in my case, unless God had initiated a search and rescue mission for my soul, I would still be lost today.

Being lost can manifest itself in many forms.

Proverbs 5 provides one illustration of what it looks like to be lost. In no uncertain terms, Solomon warns of the dangers of sexual promiscuity. Among other things, he speaks of disease (5:11), public disgrace (5:14), loss of honor (5:9), and a bitter poisonous ending to the story (5:4). He asks the rather blunt but pragmatic question: *"Why spill the water of your springs in the streets, having sex with just anyone?"* (5:16) At the end of his forthright discourse, he concludes: *"An evil man is held captive by his own sins; they are ropes that catch and hold him. He will die for lack of self-control; he will be lost because of his great foolishness"* (5:22–23).

It is the foolishness of our sin that makes us lost. And even good upstanding citizens who pay their taxes and do community service are lost when they live autonomously, refusing to acknowledge God's presence in the world and in their lives. Whether it is the starving Prodigal Son slopping around in the mud of a pig pen, or the polite, well-dressed, and well-versed intellectual atheist, everyone who has not come to the Father through Jesus Christ is lost.

Regardless of my neglect to think in these terms, God is thinking about the lost at all times. He expects his followers to do likewise.

The Jewish religious leaders of Jesus' day had many problems with the Son of Man. It peeved them that Jesus would hang out and eat with notorious sinners while assuming the role of a rabbi. In response to the complaints of the Pharisees and the teachers of the Law, Jesus told three parables about finding lost things—a lamb, a coin, and a child (Luke 15).

In each of these instructive stories, the emphasis was on the joy involved in finding that which was lost. Partying was essential—there was a gathering of friends and loved ones to celebrate the fact that the lost had been found. The three accounts drip with love, compassion, and excitement.

Even though the wayward sheep represented only one percent of the herd, the shepherd was willing to do whatever it took to find the lost lamb. Even though the woman had nine other silver coins, she furiously swept the entire house into the dark hours of the night until she found the missing one. And, even though the son had totally blown the wad and his moral integrity, the father could hardly wait to receive him back home with open arms.

It's easy to assume Jesus was speaking mainly to the masses in Luke 15. But a careful examination of these stories reveals another motive. Jesus had something very powerful to say to the self-righteous religious leaders in the crowd (represented by the older brother in the narrative). He wanted them to know that his Heavenly Father had deep compassion for the lost, even though they didn't. Not only did they lack zeal for the lost, they were clueless as to their own lost condition. This is a pathetic position to be in as a religious leader. It's no wonder Jesus referred to them as *"blind guides"* (Matthew 23:16).

Historically, this was not new. Over six centuries earlier, the religious leaders of Ezekiel's day had also failed to include the lost in their paradigm. As spiritual shepherds, they had neglected to tend to the needs of their flock, so God dealt them a scathing rebuke. The passage is long but warrants careful attention because it clarifies God's thinking on this matter as no other Scripture does. Listen to God talking.

> *You have not taken care of the weak. You have not tended the sick or bound up the injured. You have not gone looking for those who have wandered away and are lost. Instead, you have ruled them with harshness and cruelty. So my sheep have been scattered without a shepherd, and they are easy prey for any wild animal. They have wandered through all the mountains and all the hills, across the face of the earth, yet no one has gone to search for them.*

*Therefore, you shepherds, hear the word of the Lord: As
surely as I live, says the Sovereign Lord, you abandoned my
flock and left them to be attacked by every wild animal. And
though you were my shepherds, you didn't search for my
sheep when they were lost. You took care of yourselves and
left the sheep to starve. Therefore, you shepherds, hear the
word of the Lord. This is what the Sovereign Lord says: I
now consider these shepherds my enemies, and I will hold
them responsible for what has happened to my flock. I will
take away their right to feed the flock, and I will stop them
from feeding themselves. I will rescue my flock from their
mouths; the sheep will no longer be their prey.*

*For this is what the Sovereign Lord says: I myself will
search and find my sheep. I will be like a shepherd looking
for his scattered flock. I will find my sheep and rescue them
from all the places where they were scattered on that dark
and cloudy day. I will bring them back home to their own
land of Israel from among the peoples and nations. I will
feed them on the mountains of Israel and by the rivers and
in all the places where people live. Yes, I will give them
good pastureland on the high hills of Israel. There they will
lie down in pleasant places and feed in the lush pastures of
the hills. I myself will tend my sheep and give them a place
to lie down in peace, says the Sovereign Lord. I will search
for my lost ones who strayed away, and I will bring them
safely home again. I will bandage the injured and
strengthen the weak. But I will destroy those who are fat
and powerful. I will feed them, yes—feed them justice!*
(Ezekiel 34:4–16)

Can you hear the heartbeat of the Good Shepherd? Do
you grasp his thinking? Can you feel his passion? Do you
understand how much God wants to find lost souls and bring
them to a secure place and give them good things—
sustenance, rest, peace, safety, and healing?

So, what's our problem? Why are we reluctant to care
about the lost? Are we too busy? Are we too tired? Does
everything else just seem more interesting, whether it's

Monday Night Football or Dan Brown's latest novel? We appear to have no burning desire to be intentional about this matter.

Or, perhaps we hesitate to label people as *lost* for fear of violating Christ's command of *"Do not judge others"* (Matthew 7:1). We may also be reluctant because of Paul's exhortation to refrain from judging people outside the church—which he explains as God's business (1 Corinthians 5:12–13). How do we tell someone they are lost without offending them?

I'm not sure. But let's not obsess with the judging aspect. This is not about critiquing people or displaying an attitude of superiority. This is not about discouraging others. This is about love and compassion for the world. This is about empathy for fellow travelers who need a Savior. This is about coming alongside our Creator and working with him as he seeks for lost people who will begin to worship him in spirit and truth (John 4:23). This is about warning people of the travesty of gaining the whole world but losing their soul (Luke 9:25).

In the process of trying to gain something, people believe they are seeking after good things, just like the sheep who wanders away looking for food and shelter on his own. The lost are blinded by Satan; they are not deliberately trying to be lost. We need to treat all people with dignity and respect regardless of their current spiritual state.

How about this approach? Why don't we simply tell our stories and let other people tell theirs. As we invite others into our homes, feed them some good food, and invite them to talk about their lives, they themselves may discover that they are truly lost. If our lives radiate enough good Gospel light, souls in darkness may realize their current position and gain a desire to change the direction of their journey. What if our lives could create in others a hunger and thirst for God, where they want what we have?

Perhaps that's what Jesus meant in his Sermon on the Mount: *"In the same way, let your good deeds shine out for all to see, so that everyone will praise your heavenly Father"* (Matthew 5:16). When we walk in integrity and purity before God and man, the Holy Spirit can use that light to expose a sense of lostness in someone's life. Or, to use another analogy, when the light of Jesus causes the shadows from their prison bars to fall across their bodies, they finally get it.

Evangelism consists of links in a chain. God uses many people and events to bring the lost back to himself. If we want to be one of those useful links in the line, we must be thinking *lost* in order to carpe diem. It needs to be at the forefront of our minds and our prayers.

If we want to move towards a divine paradigm, we cannot be consumed with the drivel and deception of wasteful worldliness. We need to see ourselves as lost and humbly let the Savior rescue us. Then, grasping the urgency of the moment, we need to move out into the world with a sharpened spiritual perception of the lostness of humanity so that we may become useful participants in the Almighty's divine search and rescue mission.

DISCUSSION QUESTIONS

1. Why do the spiritually lost rarely realize they are lost?

2. What is the most common imagery in the Scriptures for lost humanity?

3. Why do Christians struggle to think deeply or often about the lost?

4. What is the difference between a spiritually lost homeless drug addict and a spiritually lost successful businessperson?

5. What do we learn from Luke 15 about God's attitude towards finding the lost?

6. In Ezekiel, who does God hold responsible for the unreached lost?

7. Why might a Christian hesitate to label someone as lost?

8. As the church, what approach should we use to truly make an effort to reach the lost?

Chapter 8

"Orphans and widows are particularly dear to my heart."

*"Father to the fatherless, defender of widows—
this is God, whose dwelling is holy."*

~ Psalm 68:5

Human thinking values strength. We applaud industry and independence. Those who can take care of themselves without burdening others are deemed more valuable to society than those who need assistance.

It's not part of our natural thought process to consider the marginalized or the needy around us. Life is busy and we have a hard enough time taking care of our own responsibilities and providing for our own needs.

Wealth is rather relative. Some people require a lot more than others to survive. Even so, the poverty line continues to rise, and in today's precarious economic climate, even the middle to upper middle classes feel like they are in a fiscal pinch. As we experience our own monetary and circumstantial pressures, it's easy to neglect those in even poorer situations than ourselves.

But to get lost in our own worlds and neglect the poor, the underdog, the widow, or the foreigner in an oppressive situation is to be remiss. God holds a special place in his heart for the defenseless, and he wants us to do likewise. He values the weak, and takes special notice of their hardship and affliction. To think like God is to be more perceptive to the needs of the downtrodden, and to respond timely and tangibly.

Our Creator made it very clear—*"Pure and genuine religion in the sight of God the Father means caring for orphans and widows in their distress and refusing to let the world corrupt you"* (James 1:27). There's a lot of religion being practiced in the world today, but the pure and undefiled version involves care for those in need. True religion is very practical and helpful in deficit situations. Evangelicals fear the Social Gospel—Jesus knew no other.

God selected the Jewish nation to play a very special role in the world. Among other things, they were to model proper social behaviour which included fair treatment for the underdog and protection for the defenseless. As God's chosen people, the Israelites were accountable to high expectations in these matters. Though there are dozens of specific commands given to the Jews, the common theme is justice: *"Give justice to the poor and the orphan; uphold the rights of the oppressed and the destitute"* (Psalm 82:3).

Orphans, widows, foreigners, and the poor often find themselves in situations that are unjust. It's not fair for a woman to lose her husband, especially in a culture where provision is male-dominated. It's not fair for small children to be deprived of a parent. It's not fair when circumstances bring stinging poverty into the lives of the unlucky. Repeatedly, countless foreign refugees have received unreasonable and abusive treatment from their host countries.

Indeed, throughout much of history, there has been no one to help the weak. The author of Ecclesiastes wrote, *"Again, I observed all the oppression that takes place under the sun. I saw the tears of the oppressed, with no one to comfort them. The oppressors have great power, and their victims are helpless"* (Ecclesiastes 4:1).

Today, in our more socialist Western societies with enlarged governments, there are safety nets of varying degrees to catch the disadvantaged and provide a measure of assistance; but there are still many needs. More on that later.

Consider some of the commands God gave his people regarding the oppressed. Obviously, the first priority was food. Without it, all other concerns are moot. God gave the Israelites numerous instructions to ensure that the marginalized elements of their society did not go hungry.

When you are harvesting your crops and forget to bring in a bundle of grain from your field, don't go back to get it. Leave it for the foreigners, orphans, and widows. Then the Lord your God will bless you in all you do. When you beat the olives from your olive trees, don't go over the boughs twice. Leave the remaining olives for the foreigners, orphans, and widows. When you gather the grapes in your vineyard, don't glean the vines after they are picked. Leave the remaining grapes for the foreigners, orphans, and widows (Deuteronomy 24:19–21).

And again, *"When you harvest the crops of your land, do not harvest the grain along the edges of your fields, and do not pick up what the harvesters drop. Leave it for the poor and the foreigners living among you. I am the Lord your God"* (Leviticus 23:22).

God instructed his people to be deliberately careless in their harvesting technique so the needy could scrounge up their portion. Notice, this is not a handout; the underdogs were still expected to do the work of gathering and harvesting themselves. Thus, the dignity of the disadvantaged remained intact.

On top of this, a special offering was to be collected and given to the needy. *"Every third year you must offer a special tithe of your crops. In this year of the special tithe you must give your tithes to the Levites, foreigners, orphans, and widows, so that they will have enough to eat in your towns"* (Deuteronomy 26:12) and *"then the Lord will bless you in all your work"* (Deuteronomy 14:29).

But God also told the Jews to make sure the poor and underprivileged were included in the celebrations accompanying their three main annual feasts (Passover, Feast of Harvest, Feast of Booths – Deuteronomy 16:1–15). It was important for the widows, orphans, aliens, and the destitute to be a part of these happy times of rejoicing, as opposed to being disenfranchised non-participants, gloomily looking in from the outside. They were to feel every bit as much of the party as the average well-to-do citizen.

Such benevolence was not without a logical basis. When thinking about the needs of the underprivileged, the Israelites were encouraged to reflect on their own oppression and captivity in the past (Deuteronomy 16:11–12). They were once the underdogs, dwelling as aliens in Egypt for 400 years. Before the grace of God was fully realized through their entrance into the Promised Land, they were hard done by and lacking. Historically, they knew what it was like to be in need, to be dependent on others' generosity.

Because of the vulnerability of the underprivileged, God also warned his people not to take advantage of them in any way. The Law specifically commanded: *"You must not exploit a widow or an orphan"* (Exodus 22:22). Solomon added, *"Don't take the land of defenseless orphans"* (Proverbs 23:10). The prophet Zechariah agreed: *"Do not oppress widows, orphans, foreigners, and the poor. And do not scheme against each other"* (Zechariah 7:10).

On the contrary, God encourages his followers to be generous with the needy:

> *But if there are any poor Israelites in your towns when you arrive in the land the Lord your God is giving you, do not be hard-hearted or tightfisted toward them. Instead, be generous and lend them whatever they need. Do not be mean-spirited and refuse someone a loan because the year for canceling debts is close at hand. If you refuse to make the loan and the needy person cries out to the Lord, you will be considered guilty of sin. Give generously to the poor, not*

*grudgingly, for the Lord your God will bless you in
everything you do. There will always be some in the land
who are poor. That is why I am commanding you to share
freely with the poor and with other Israelites in need*
(Deuteronomy 15:7–11).

It was considered heartless to take the last meager
possessions of the poor to guarantee a loan. *"True justice must
be given to foreigners living among you and to orphans, and
you must never accept a widow's garment as security for her
debt"* (Deuteronomy 24:17). Repeatedly, it is noted that the
wicked do such tyrannical things. *"They take the orphan's
donkey and demand the widow's ox as security for a loan"*
(Job 24:3). And, even more horribly, *"They kill widows and
foreigners and murder orphans"* (Psalm 94:6).

It is particularly treacherous when the leaders of the
country are the greatest offenders. This was the case in Israel
when Isaiah was prophesying. He wrote, *"Your leaders are
rebels, the companions of thieves. All of them love bribes and
demand payoffs, but they refuse to defend the cause of orphans
or fight for the rights of widows"* (Isaiah 1:23). The same
problem was going on in Ezekiel's day: *"Foreigners are
forced to pay for protection. Orphans and widows are
wronged and oppressed among you"* (Ezekiel 22:7).

The Bible says that such negligent and abusive behavior
towards widows, orphans, and the poor shows that the
offender(s) truly have no fear of God (Malachi 3:5). Solomon
said, *"Those who oppress the poor insult their Maker"* (Proverbs
14:31). This is a precarious position to be in, for God declares
himself to be their protector and defender (Psalm 68:5). *"But I
will protect the orphans who remain among you. Your widows,
too, can depend on me for help"* (Jeremiah 49:11). The Psalmist
concurred: *"The Lord protects the foreigners among us. He
cares for the orphans and widows, but he frustrates the plans of
the wicked"* (Psalm 146:9). It was a well-known fact that the
Torah specifically declared: *"Cursed is anyone who denies
justice to foreigners, orphans, or widows"* (Deuteronomy 27:19).

Solomon wrote, *"Don't rob the poor just because you can, or exploit the needy in court. For the Lord is their defender. He will ruin anyone who ruins them"* (Proverbs 22:22–23). Hosea agreed: *"In you alone do the orphans find mercy"* (Hosea 14:3). David expressed his frustration with the temporary successes of the wicked, but he knew the helpless would eventually get their justice.

> *The helpless put their trust in you. You defend the orphans. Lord, you know the hopes of the helpless. Surely you will hear their cries and comfort them. You will bring justice to the orphans and the oppressed, so mere people can no longer terrify them* (Psalm 10:14b,17–18).

Scripture paints a picture of a coming judgment when the wicked will be held accountable for their improper behaviour. At that time, wrongs will be righted. Sometimes the judgment sounds local and imminent:

> *What sorrow awaits the unjust judges and those who issue unfair laws. They deprive the poor of justice and deny the rights of the needy among my people. They prey on widows and take advantage of orphans. What will you do when I punish you?* (Isaiah 10:1–3a)

Other times, the judgment sounds more general, apocalyptic, and eternal:

> *"At that time I will put you on trial. I am eager to witness against all sorcerers and adulterers and liars. I will* speak *against those who cheat employees of their wages, who oppress widows and orphans, or who deprive the foreigners living among you of justice, for these people do not fear me,"* says the Lord of Heaven's Armies (Malachi 3:5).

Either way, the mind of God regarding this issue is unequivocal. He is dedicated to the cause of the disadvantaged and will make us pay if we don't address their needs or if we take advantage of the down-trodden.

The prophet Jeremiah ministered at a time in Judah's history when there was great need for national repentance, starting with the king. Through his prophet, God clearly specified that any form of repentance must be accompanied by reparations in the area of neglecting the needy.

> *Listen to this message from the Lord, you king of Judah, sitting on David's throne. Let your attendants and your people listen, too. This is what the Lord says: Be fair-minded and just. Do what is right! Help those who have been robbed; rescue them from their oppressors. Quit your evil deeds! Do not mistreat foreigners, orphans, and widows. Stop murdering the innocent! If you obey me, there will always be a descendant of David sitting on the throne here in Jerusalem...But if you refuse to pay attention to this warning, I swear by my own name, says the Lord, that this palace will become a pile of rubble* (Jeremiah 22:2–5).

If these social crimes of neglect and abuse were not remedied, there would be no deliverance from their enemies:

> *I will be merciful only if you stop your evil thoughts and deeds and start treating each other with justice; only if you stop exploiting foreigners, orphans, and widows; only if you stop your murdering; and only if you stop harming yourselves by worshiping idols. Then I will let you stay in this land that I gave to your ancestors to keep forever* (Jeremiah 7:5–7).

Ultimately, failure to think like God in this situation brought about the ruination of a great nation. Who is to say that the same thing cannot happen today in the twenty-first century?

What is God holding us accountable for at this time? What can we do to correct blatant injustices? Our legal system still favors the wealthy. When was the last time a member of a poor minority group won an appeal in a high profile legal case?

What does God think about Canada's response to the 937 German Jewish refugees aboard the M.S. St. Louis that were refused entry into our country in 1939? What does God think about the treatment of black soldiers by the American military establishment during the Vietnam Conflict? And what about the contemptible behavior in the Japanese internment camps during World War II? Is there something I can do today about the abuse of human rights in the Sudan? What role should I play in defending the rights of the unborn or in providing better care for those young girls who opt to keep their children?

Sometimes the needs are less dramatic, but equally vital. Perhaps you have a widow in your neighborhood that could use your help with lawn care, snow removal, home repair, or an occasional ride to the grocery store. Maybe it's time to start sponsoring some children overseas. Possibly, a short-term mission trip might illuminate your understanding of Third World poverty. Perhaps it's time to make a more meaningful connection with your 'new' neighbor that you still refer to as 'foreign', even though he's been your neighbor for two years already. Maybe you could play a surrogate supportive role for a child down the street that has lost a parent.

To get better at this, we must learn to see the needs of the disadvantaged through a more perceptive lens. For instance, it may be helpful to broaden our scope of the terms widows and orphans. Divorce continues to ravage our culture, leaving many single mothers or fathers with the daunting task of trying to raise their children on skimpy assets. To the lone surviving adult in the family, there may be very little economic and psychological difference between the woman whose husband died and the one whose husband walked away with his twenty-two-year-old secretary. Both have suffered wrenching loss. Both have incredible needs. Both may have children that could benefit from the input of another discerning and caring adult.

Are you a salesperson? Do you resist the temptation to take advantage of the elderly who may be a bit too trusting and naïve? Are you involved in ministries where widows' dollars could be easily manipulated into your coffers? Are you in a position of substantial wealth and influence? Do you think carefully about how your corporate or managerial decisions may be affecting the less fortunate in your organization or your greater sphere of influence?

You do not want to stand before the Judge one day and declare that you didn't realize the detrimental impact of some of your monetary and management choices. You need to hear the voices of those who feel oppressed by your decisions, even if the charges are debatable.

I understand the entrepreneurial world is complicated. There is a balance between creating jobs for the masses and making profit. I get it. Many people wouldn't even have a job had you not created the employment opportunity in the first place. Certainly, there is some truth to Adam Smith's principle of the 'invisible hand.' But beware—you do not want to be lax or slipshod. This is an area for which God feels great passion. He has spoken unquestionably about it in his Word and there can be no mistake that oppression and abuse will one day come to light and accountability enforced.

Are your deliberations and actions characterized by compassion, mercy, and justice? Do you take notice of defenseless people *"in their distress"* (James 1:27) and contemplate what you might do to alleviate their anxiety? Or are you obsessed with your own problems, oblivious to the needs around you? The New Testament command to the church is clear: *"Take care of any widow who has no one else to care for her"* (1 Timothy 5:3).

But sometimes the issue can be more subtle. Churches and social organizations may not openly afflict orphans, widows, foreigners, and the poor, but they marginalize them by their structure or unspoken attitudes. Church groups dominated by young married couples can unintentionally but inadvertently disenfranchise singles, creating that lousy feeling that they don't really belong or that they're second class citizens. Unintentionally, educational institutions can discourage children with non-traditional or complicated family arrangements by failing to be sensitive to their special needs.

We still make excuses though. Given the rise of terrorist activity worldwide, we may remain reticent to embrace foreigners with open arms. We may parallel the rise of gang violence in our cities with the presence of more 'foreigners' in 'our' land (even though the only non-foreigners in North America are the First Nations Peoples). Because of the manner in which they help each other out financially, we may be quick to judge immigrants as routinely gaining an unfair advantage in what we deem to be 'our' country. I know these issues are complex, but they are still not an excuse for xenophobic speech and behavior. There are foreigners in our world who need our help. There are refugees from war-torn developing nations arriving daily in our cities.

And what about the poor? Well, we can easily be tempted to rationalize our non-involvement in their plight because we perceive their situations to be self-imposed by personal sin or recklessness. Whether or not that is the case is not significant. God commands us to be open-handed to the needs of the poor. *"Blessed are those who help the poor"* (Proverbs 14:21). The Psalmist says that one who fears the Lord will *"share freely and give generously to those in need"* (Psalm 112:9). The grace we bestow on them is a picture of the grace God has bestowed upon our lives, both spiritual and financial. The person who truly understands who they would be without Jesus Christ tends to be more liberal in their generosity to the destitute.

I pray that it may never be us who are the rich and inattentive, the ones that Jeremiah described thus:

> *"They are fat and sleek, and there is no limit to their wicked deeds. They refuse to provide justice to orphans and deny the rights of the poor. Should I not punish them for this?" says the Lord. "Should I not avenge myself against such a nation?"* (Jeremiah 5:28–29)

The New Testament equates proper treatment of the poor with real Christianity.

> *If someone has enough money to live well and sees a brother or sister in need but shows no compassion—how can God's love be in that person? Dear children, let's not merely say that we love each other; let us show the truth by our actions* (1 John 3:17–18).

Genuine Christian faith demands genuine compassionate action.

The message is quite simple. When you think like God, you behave like a good person. *"Learn to do good. Seek justice. Help the oppressed. Defend the cause of orphans. Fight for the rights of widows"* (Isaiah 1:17). At the end of our earthly lives, may we be able to echo the words of the righteous Job who testified, *"For I assisted the poor in their need and the orphans who required help"* (Job 29:12). *"Have I been stingy with my food and refused to share it with orphans? No, from childhood I have cared for orphans like a father, and all my life I have cared for widows"* (Job 31:17–18).

DISCUSSION QUESTIONS

1. Describe God's attitude towards widows, orphans, oppressed foreigners, and the poor.

2. How were the Israelites to care for the needy in their community?

3. What was the basis for this 'socialist' mindset (#2)?

4. Why is it easy for Westerners to overlook the downtrodden?

5. What is the outcome for those who deliberately abuse the needy?

6. What role should a Christian play in response to major social injustices in the world?

7. How might believers follow after God's heart in this matter within their own neighborhoods and churches?

8. "Evangelicals fear the Social Gospel—Jesus knew no other." Agree or disagree.

Chapter 9

"No, seriously, my clock's not broken."

*"But you must not forget this one thing, dear friends:
A day is like a thousand years to the Lord,
and a thousand years is like a day."*

~ 2 Peter 3:8

Some people live by their own clocks. I have a friend, let's call him Bob (seriously, not his real name). He lives on BST—Bob's Stubborn Time. You can't rush Bob. He arrives when *he* is ready, regardless of the real scheduled time of the event.

But it's not just people who have diverse attitudes towards time; even cultures view time differently. Some civilizations are more laid back, while others are more rushed and uptight about deadlines, schedules, and start times. Generally, Western civilization runs rigidly by the clock. We want to know when things are going to happen and how long they will last, and we don't like to wait longer than necessary.

I think it's fair to say that humans in the West are impatient. We want things to happen sooner than later. We like to execute our plans promptly once they become clear in our minds. We scurry here and there, hoping the current event finishes fast enough to make it to the next one.

I wonder why we're in such a hurry. Where are we going that demands such haste?

As parents, we desire our young children to grow up quickly. We press them to walk, talk, and use the toilet independently. We fret when little three-year-old Alex still struggles to get it in the pot. When developmental progress is smooth and successful, we brag to other parents about how advanced our children are for their age. We tend to see a lot of life as a competition that must be won, with a special prize for the one who can do it the fastest.

We strive to pay off our houses and get out of debt quickly. We do our utmost to be financially savvy so that we can retire sooner. But once we reach that point, what do we see awaiting us as we pull ourselves over the precipice? A busier highway than the one we were previously on making our way to retirement.

Again, what's the point? What is this final destination we are striving for as we industriously stroke items off our lists? Why are we in such a rush? What is so urgent? Might we actually be guilty of going nowhere fast?

In contrast to the human notion of time efficiency, God seems to take too long at just about everything. His promises are true, but their fulfillment may not arrive according to our desired schedule.

In the Book of Genesis, God promised to make Abraham the father of a great nation, even though, at the time, he was fairly old and had no children. By faith, he believed God's promise. But after ten years and no baby, Abraham got fed up waiting for God to deliver. The Lord seemed to be taking too long. His growing impatience with God led him to fall into a scheme of offspring production that involved having an affair with his wife's servant—thus came Ishmael.

But we can't be too hard on Abraham. Thirteen years after the birth of Ishmael, God had still not given him a true heir through Sarah. And yet the Lord commanded Abraham to *"serve me faithfully and live a blameless life"* (Genesis 17:1). The Lord told Abraham to continue to walk in holiness even though, as of yet, there was nothing tangible to show for his faith. Twenty-four years after moving to Canaan, Sarah was still barren.

Patiently waiting on the Lord can be quite challenging. Impatience on our part can cause us to do foolish things. Ishmael was Abraham's attempt to fabricate the work of God in his own life. Perhaps he even thought his solution was a way of helping God out of a jam.

Humans often do this. We create earthly solutions to lingering problems or unresolved issues and then ascribe the outcome to God's sovereignty. Instead of patiently waiting on the Lord, we move in to help him out.

How often have young people prematurely rushed into wedding plans instead of waiting for God's specially chosen partner for their lives? How often have we made a hasty career or residential move just because we thought we were in a rut or needed a change? These situations are often devoid of the Lord's leading; truthfully, they are just our independent attempts to respond to the angst in our souls at moments when we deemed God to be aloof or asleep.

One of the more dangerous avenues to explore when fabricating the Lord's work in your life is the vocation of full-time Christian ministry. Across North America, countless youth and associate pastors in their early twenties have been chewed up and spit out because they were considered inept in their calling to serve in very challenging church ministries. And it's largely not their fault that many beginning pastors disappoint us—they are too young.

By God's design, Jesus himself had to wait until he was thirty years old before he started his ministry. Think about it. If the Son of God had to wait until he was thirty before he moved into the public eye to perform full-time ministry, how old do you think we should be before we get immersed into serious Christian leadership roles?

Moses trained for forty years in Pharaoh's court and spent another forty hiding in the desert before he emerged as Israel's deliverer. We can only imagine how confused Moses must have been, tending his father-in-law's sheep in the wilderness, knowing all along that God had most likely prepared him to be something more than a shepherd. For four decades, he had to wake up every morning and process his perplexing circumstances. He had no idea that he would have to wait until he was eighty before he would see the burning bush and be called to return to Egypt as a deliverer.

The Apostle Paul also had to wait a considerable length of time before starting his full-time ministry. Even after all his biblical training as a Pharisee, and his own special revelations from God, it appears he had to wait eleven years after his conversion before the Lord launched him out on his first missionary journey.[15] During that time, he was anxious to get out there and preach the Gospel, but God-ordained circumstances kept him close to home while the Lord continued to prepare him for future greatness.

This pattern of patience and waiting upon the Lord is common throughout the Scriptures.

Even though they all appeared to be women of devout faith, several mothers in the Bible had to wait many years before the Lord finally gave them a child: Sarah – Isaac, Rebekkah – Jacob, Rachel – Joseph, wife of Manoah – Samson, Hannah – Samuel, and, Elizabeth – John the Baptist. In every case, the profound role played by the children, once they did arrive, testifies to the blessing of waiting for the Lord's sovereign timing.

Joseph spent about eleven years in a dungeon as a falsely-accused prisoner before being released to lead Egypt through one of the worst agricultural crises in its history.

David assumed his role as monarch of Judah twenty-five years after Samuel had anointed him as king.[16] And much of that time was spent running and hiding from a jealous King

---

[15] Cited September 18, 2009 http://www.biblestudy.org/apostlepaul/timeline1.html

[16] Cited September 18, 2009 http://www.livingstonesclass.org/Archive/DavidChronologyGross.pdf

Saul. David's life leading up to his coronation was a time of great confusion, frustration, and at times, solitude. But through loneliness and struggle, David learned to fully depend on God.

According to the account of the birth of Christ in Luke's Gospel, temple ministers Simeon and Anna were senior citizens who had waited decades for the coming of the Messiah. There must have been periods in their lives when they wondered whether or not God was actually going to fulfill the prophecies.

Believers throughout history have longed for the return of Christ, wondering when God will finally act. Almost 2000 years ago, the Apostle Paul gave the impression that Christ's return was close at hand, but dozens of generations have passed since that time without seeing it.

The Apostle Peter addressed this matter in his second epistle. In response to scoffers who claim the long delay means Christ is never coming back, Peter writes:

But you must not forget this one thing, dear friends: A day is like a thousand years to the Lord, and a thousand years is like a day. The Lord isn't really being slow about his promise, as some people think. No, he is being patient for your sake. He does not want anyone to be destroyed, but wants everyone to repent (2 Peter 3:8–9).

He is not slow; he is patient and kind and has a merciful plan that gives more people a chance to repent. God runs on his own time and humans will always be frustrated with that fact until they learn to submit to the Almighty and trust that he and his plans are good.

Even the martyred saints under the altar in Revelation 6 are impatient with God's delay in punishing the wicked; they want vengeance, now.

When the Lamb broke the fifth seal, I saw under the altar the souls of all who had been martyred for the word of God and for being faithful in their testimony. They shouted to the Lord and said, "O Sovereign Lord, holy and true, how long before you judge the people who belong to this world and avenge our blood for what they have done to us?" Then a white robe was given to each of them. And they were told to rest a little longer until the full number of their brothers and sisters—their fellow servants of Jesus who were to be martyred—had joined them (Revelation 6:9–11).

Oh, how we want the Lord to get moving! We deeply desire that he bring back our wayward children, soon. We want our healings to arrive swiftly and our problems to dissipate today. We wish he would confirm right now that our latest business venture has his approval. We can hardly handle delay. God's timing can seem so slow.

But also within the sovereignty of God, some things seem to end too abruptly. King Hezekiah felt that way when the Lord told him, through the prophet Isaiah, to put his affairs in order for he was about to die. Hezekiah assumed the Lord's clock was wrong so he cried and pleaded for more time, reminding God that he had been a good boy all his life. God gave him fifteen more years; but during that time Hezekiah foolishly showed off all the royal treasures to the Babylonians (those who would one day come and steal them) and birthed a little boy, Manasseh, who would one day grow up to be the most wicked king in Israel's history. An analysis of Hezekiah's life leads one to conclude that he should have died on time.

God's clock was keeping, and continues to keep, perfect time. When the good die young, the human mind calculates that something is wrong in the functioning of the Universe. In the mind of God, there is much more to life than this earthly matinee. By man's standards, many followers of the Lord disappear too early.

John the Baptist was removed from the scene just as quickly as he appeared. James, the brother of John, was murdered in the prime of his fruitful work as an apostle. Even the public ministry of Jesus seems too short. Why would God remove him from the Earth after only three years of service?

Couldn't Jesus have done more good for people with a longer earthly ministry?

From a human perspective, it can seem like God's timing is totally out of whack. But it's not. His clock is perfect. We are the ones who need to adjust our watches. We are the ones who see everything from such a limited vantage point.

On that day, when we are remade into the likeness of Christ, we will get it. We will finally be able to echo the words of the Apostle Paul: *"Now we see things imperfectly as in a cloudy mirror, but then we will see everything with perfect clarity. All that I know now is partial and incomplete, but then I will know everything completely, just as God now knows me completely"* (1 Corinthians 13:12).

So why does God keep us guessing now with his timing? Why does he make us wait? I can think of several reasons. Obviously, waiting for God's plan provides us with the best possible course for our lives. Schemes that are prematurely forced by our hands are sub-standard at best, and at times, disastrous.

Besides, I think we learn more from the wait than from the actual fulfillment of the desired event or request. Once we are healed, delivered, or our prayers answered, we may be tempted to forget the Lord, or think that we rescued ourselves from our plight.

As well, it is in the waiting that we learn to trust him, even when it doesn't seem to make sense. We learn to depend less on human reason and embrace the mystery of a sovereign God. And when we are forced to wait for the Lord, we often discover new purposes for our lives that never occurred to us when things were going smoothly.

What's more, waiting patiently for the Lord is a way to show God how much we love him. Even if our hopes and dreams are not fulfilled, or something good ends too early, or someone is taken from us prematurely, we are content to be in the presence of our Lord. Waiting on the Lord also reminds us that we are dependent on him for everything—every breath, every heartbeat, every sane thought.

But waiting is hard, and not for the faint of heart. It takes courage. *"Wait patiently for the Lord. Be brave and courageous. Yes, wait patiently for the Lord"* (Psalm 27:14). Sometimes it seems like God is not doing what we think he should. Sometimes the bad guys are getting away with stuff. In response to this, the Psalmist exhorts us to *"be still in the presence of the Lord, and wait patiently for him to act. Don't worry about evil people who prosper or fret about their wicked schemes"* (Psalm 37:7).

You see, believers who learn to tough it out and wait for God's timing do not lose out in the end. Just look at the promises God has for those who wait patiently for him and his purposes.

> *Do you not know? Have you not heard? The Everlasting God, the LORD, the Creator of the ends of the earth does not become weary or tired. His understanding is inscrutable. He gives strength to the weary, and to him who lacks might He increases power. Though youths grow weary and tired, and vigorous young men stumble badly, yet those who wait for the LORD will gain new strength; they will mount up with wings like eagles, they will run and not get tired, they will walk and not become weary* (Isaiah 40:28–31 NASB).

And how about this verse? *"For since the world began, no ear has heard, and no eye has seen a God like you, who works for those who wait for him!"* (Isaiah 64:4)

If you want God on your side, you must respect him as the quarterback of the team. He will make the decisions regarding where the ball goes next. As a wide receiver, even if you get into the open, you may not get the pass. But you can't lose faith in your quarterback. We need to say like Micah, *"As for me, I look to the Lord for help. I wait confidently for God to save me, and my God will certainly hear me"* (Micah 7:7).

Sometimes, our sinful nature causes our vision to get out of focus. We get confused about our needs and our wants. We think we know what we want; but when God, by his permissive will, ends up giving it to us, we quickly realize that we don't really want it after all. The children of Israel discovered this when they whined for some meat in the wilderness. *"So he gave them what they asked for, but sent a wasting disease upon them"* (Psalm 106:15 NIV).

No, I think we're much safer waiting for God's schedule, patiently surrendering our trust to the Maker of time.

But there is also great irony in our waiting for God's timing. When we think God is dragging his heels, we may actually be the variable that is slowing down the equation. Sometimes God is waiting for *us* to take some proper action before he will act. He does not force himself upon us. If we feel like being independent, he may let us wander until we come back to our senses. Perhaps Isaiah had this in mind when he said, *"So the Lord must wait for you to come to him so he can show you his love and compassion. For the Lord is a faithful God. Blessed are those who wait for his help"* (Isaiah 30:18).

My mind goes to the image of a little boy and his father building a go-cart. It starts off just fine. Both parties are having a good time, enjoying working together. But as the venture drags on, the son gets increasingly impatient for the project to be completed. Continually he asks his father if the cart is done yet. Repeatedly the father says, "No". The child does not understand. They have been building this thing for weeks. How can it not be ready? The father, however, as the chief technician, understands the proper timing. He's not going to send his precious son down a hill in a cart with no brakes or a steering mechanism that still needs some tweaking. The father knows when the cart will truly be ready.

Repeatedly we make inane judgments about life from our purely human perspective. The Sovereign God of the Universe, unmoved by our whining and impatience, continues to work out his divine plan according to his schedule.

God, and God alone, knows when everything should happen. Even Jesus, in his role as son, does not know when he is going to return to Earth (Mark 13:32). But our Heavenly Father, with unfathomable wisdom and immeasurable love, is weaving together the storyline of countless souls into an earthly tale that will bring him praise and honor and *"bring many children into glory"* (Hebrews 2:10).

So may we, with the Psalmist, be able to say with full confidence, *"Let all that I am wait quietly before God, for my hope is in him"* (Psalm 62:5).

DISCUSSION QUESTIONS

1. Why are people in the West typically in a hurry?

2. How would you describe Abraham's experience with God's timing?

3. What are some of the things we do because of impatience with God's timing?

4. What is the appropriate age to enter a major leadership role in Christian ministry? Why?

5. Which biblical characters besides Abraham had their faith tested as they waited for God's timing?

6. Describe some situations where we might deem God's timing to be too early or too fast.

7. Why does God keep us guessing with regard to his timing?

8. Sometimes when we are 'waiting for the Lord to act', there's another issue at play. Explain.

Chapter 10

"You might want to pay more attention to conspiracy theories."

*"This great dragon—the ancient serpent called the devil,
or Satan, the one deceiving the whole world—
was thrown down to the earth with all his angels."*

~ Revelation 12:9

"The complete lack of evidence is the surest sign that
the conspiracy is working."

(anonymous)

Did Lee Harvey Oswald truly act as a lone crazed gunman in the assassination of JFK? Were there aspects of 9–11 that were actually a scheme to cover up a massive money-making venture as well as a plot to forever change the nature of security in the Western world? Did the Americans really land on the moon in the summer of 1969, just in time to fulfill President Kennedy's 1961 prophecy? Do the Illuminati play a directive role in contemporary world politics?

The mainstream modern mind is intrigued by conspiracy theories and their sinister interpretation of history. When something seems a little fishy, we want to know the truth. Curiosity drives us to find out what's been covered up and who had the power to do so. And it may not be merely a hunger for truth—we can be shamefully egotistical.

Knowledge of the conspiracy makes us feel smarter than
others. It establishes us as members of an elite group, those
who really know what's going on.

Of course, the scientific community and academia view
conspiracy theories with skepticism and authorities ridicule
them as speculative, outlandish, irrational, and unsubstantiated.
The phrase itself has come to be used largely in a derogatory
and dismissive fashion, tossing aside crazed cranks that
supposedly belong to the lunatic fringe.

Now, while an obsessive paranoia and pre-occupation
with conspiracy theories could be deemed unhealthy and
unproductive, we should be careful not to blow them off
prematurely as stupid and silly just because they sound far-
fetched. To think like God might necessitate the consideration
of more cover-ups and conspiracies than one would normally
think.

What is conspiracy theory? It is the belief that groups
within the Establishment have secretly met together to plan an
unlawful or wrongful act, usually in an attempt to gain
something for themselves or deprive the People of something,
whether it be power, money, or freedom. Political scientist
Michael Barkun has categorized three types of conspiracies:
event conspiracy like the Kennedy assassination; *systemic
conspiracy* like those supposedly of the Freemasons, the
Illuminati, or international communism; and, *superconspiracy*
where multiple conspiracies are linked together hierarchically
in complex ways.[17]

From another perspective, conspiracy theory could be
considered a search for truth. At the heart of the movement is
a belief that, in contrast to the official position published by
those in authority, the real story has an alternate and seedier
interpretation. It is also a belief that those in authority have
something to gain by covering up the true tale of events. Or,
perhaps those in authority do not believe the general public

---

[17] Cited April 6, 2010 at http://en.wikipedia.org/wiki/Conspiracy_theory

can handle the truth for whatever reason, thus creating the need for a cover-up.

Regardless, conspiracies mask the truth. They are about deception. God-like thinkers have reason to doubt the official explanations of world authorities because the *"god of this age"* (2 Corinthians 4:4) is also called a deceiver (Revelation 12:9). Jesus called Satan a *"murderer"* and *"the father of lies"* (John 8:44 NIV). No truth resides in our supreme spiritual enemy. In the Garden of Eden, Satan used deception to gain power over the world system. Consequently, he has used his authority to infiltrate the world with his evil nature. The very same lust and pride that the devil used to fool Eve centuries ago still dominates the world system today (1 John 2:16).

And so we have a world system in operation that is run by the master deceiver of all time. Knowing this, why would we expect anything to be truthful or transparent? Because Satan influences the minds and motives of many rich and powerful people who run the world and control the media, perhaps we are being fed more lies than we could ever imagine.

Interestingly, most people tend to be trusting creatures. They look upon conspiracy theories with disdain or even mockery. They may even be offended by cautious or questioning minds that, to them, appear to be foolishly hunting for demons in every closet. Conspiracy-minded individuals are caricatured as fearful and frenetic psychos like Mel Gibson's character in Warner Brothers' 1997 film *Conspiracy Theory*.

When political or media authorities offer the official explanation of a catastrophic event, the initial reaction is not for people to run wildly, looking for another version of the story. No. At the outset, we take the explanation at face value and proceed. Over time, however, as cracks begin to appear in the authorized version, people become suspicious and start to ask revealing questions.

For instance, it is a well-known fact that the majority of Americans do not believe the Warren Commission's explanation for the assassination of John F. Kennedy. The nonsense in *The Magic Bullet Theory* alone renders the official explanation ridiculous (i.e. that one bullet, remaining pristine, severely injured Kennedy and caused multiple wounds to Governor Connelly). In his final public words before his death, President Gerald Ford, a key member on the Warren Commission, said their investigation was compromised by CIA interference, hiding or destroying potentially damaging information. Ford himself admitted that there "conceivably could have been a conspiracy to kill JFK."[18]

The point of this discussion is not to get into a thorough analysis of any of these events in question—that would be impractical if not insane—but to show that conspiracy musings may not be as crazy as once thought. After all, the Bible is full of conspiracies.

In the Old Testament, Joseph's brothers secretly conspired to rid him from their lives, and then lied to their father for twenty years about their dirty little secret. King Saul covertly schemed to gain support for the murder of his rival David. In the days of Jewish captivity, jealous Persian palace officials conspired against Daniel in an attempt to bring about his demise. In Jesus' day, Jewish leaders conspired to get the Romans to kill the Messiah. And in the early years of the church, the Apostle Paul often spoke of his enemies' plots to conspire against him.

Perhaps the clearest biblical illustration of a conspiracy in action is what happened after the resurrection of Christ. Jesus rose from the dead just like he said—the Romans authorities and the Jewish religious establishment were in for a world of embarrassment. Matthew tells the story:

> *As the women were on their way, some of the guards went into the city and told the leading priests what had happened. A meeting with the elders was called, and they*

---

[18] Cited April 6, 2010 http://www.crimemagazine.com/former-president-ford-admits-cia-compromised-warren-commissions-probe-jfk-assassination

decided to give the soldiers a large bribe. They told the
soldiers, "You must say, 'Jesus' disciples came during the
night while we were sleeping, and they stole his body.' If the
governor hears about it, we'll stand up for you so you won't
get in trouble." So the guards accepted the bribe and said
what they were told to say. Their story spread widely among
the Jews, and they still tell it today (Matthew 28:11–15).

The people with the power and the money had something
to lose if the truth was exposed. So they secretly met together,
paid off the appropriate characters, and then produced an
official version of the resurrection 'hoax'. They propagated
the lie and it stuck. The conspiracy was so effective, over
thirty years later the yarn was still being spun during the
writing of Matthew's Gospel. In fact, this lie has survived into
modern times and is still used by skeptics today to refute
Christ's resurrection.

Another conspiracy theme in the Scriptures is found in the
work of the satanic trinity in the Book of Revelation.
Contemporary conspiracy theorists who speak of an
impending New World Order of international unity are only
echoing what the Apostle John spoke of 1900 years ago. God
has revealed in his Word that a satanically inspired anti-Christ
with the assistance of a false prophet will establish a one-
world government and economy in the end times (Revelation
13; 17–18). The formation of this world order will be based on
deception of the masses (2 John 7; Revelation 13:14; 19:20).

Since this has been Satan's plan from the beginning, it is
believable that throughout history he has inspired many
political and economic organizations that will make this end
times transition more fluid and natural (e.g. Federal Reserve
System, IMF, Bilderberg Group, United Nations, European
Union, World Bank, Council on Foreign Relations, Trilateral
Commission). Satan may not be behind all of these groups, but
if international union is where we are headed, they can't hurt
his ultimate conspiracy plan. Even a brief examination of the
state of world affairs would lead the simplest of observers to

conclude that never have the concept and logistics of a one-world government seemed more plausible than in this generation.

Certainly, history has taught us that conspiracy thought is not just speculation and theory. Many conspiracies of the rich and powerful are now common knowledge, having been exposed through investigative research. A few examples would include: the Dreyfuss Affair of 1894 where the French government covered up the innocence of a Jewish soldier falsely incarcerated for treason; the Gleiwitz Incident of August 1939, part of twenty-one maneuvers within Operation Himmler that attempted to give the appearance of Polish aggression against Germany on the eve of World War II; Operation Mockingbird, a secret CIA campaign to influence domestic and foreign media since the 1950's; Project MK-ULTRA, a covert, illegal CIA human research program involving the surreptitious use of many kinds of mind-altering drugs on unknowing American citizens; Watergate of the early 1970's; the Iran-Contra Affair of the mid-1980's; Switzerland's Secret File Scandal that exposed the fact that the Swiss Justice and Police department had illegally gathered secret files on one-seventh of their entire population through clandestine surveillance; and, the Niger Uranium Forgeries of 2001—fake documents used to convict Sadam Hussein of buying radioactive materials to build weapons of mass destruction.

Besides these and other well established historical schemes and cover-ups, there is a growing suspicion about the truth of many official party lines including the American government's explanation of 9–11, the origin of AIDS, pharmaceutical companies controlling the dissemination of natural and alternative medicines, global warming, oil industry shortages, cancer research, big oil and gas firms suppressing electric car technologies for the past one hundred years, the mysterious elimination of Canada's high tech Avro Arrow jet program, and the deaths of many high profile individuals like Abraham

Lincoln, Franz Ferdinand, Marilyn Monroe, Malcolm X, Martin Luther King Jr., and Robert Kennedy…just to name a few.

One of the more common speculative topics of conspiracy discussion, especially since the rise of Dan Brown novels, centers on the potential role of the Illuminati in world control and domination.

> The Illuminati…is a name that refers to several groups, both historical and modern, and both real and fictitious. Historically, it refers specifically to the Bavarian Illuminati, an Enlightenment-era secret society founded on May 1, 1776. In modern times it is also used to refer to a purported conspiratorial organization which acts as a shadowy "power behind the throne", allegedly controlling world affairs through present day governments and corporations, usually as a modern incarnation or continuation of the Bavarian Illuminati. In this context, Illuminati is often used in reference to a New World Order. Many conspiracy theorists believe the Illuminati are the masterminds behind events that will lead to the establishment of such a New World Order.[19]

Well, we sure don't know much for sure. But I guess that's the point. If we did know much, the conspiracy would not be working. The point of the plan is to keep the plan a secret.

Now, when you hang out at the suspicious end of the spectrum, things can get a little crazy. It's hard to believe anyone is speaking the truth. There is always a plausible motive for a cover-up. Lust and/or pride could easily convince the powerful to hide the truth. But, on the other hand, if we assume that all conspiracies are wild hoaxes, we are presuming that everyone is telling the truth— always. This seems a bit naïve. Experience tells us, and human nature confirms, that this cannot be the case.

Conspiracies imply that there is more than meets the eye, that there are sinister forces at work in the events around us.

---

[19] Cited May 18, 2010 at http://en.wikipedia.org/wiki/Illuminati

As believers, why should this surprise us? In fact, should we not expect it since the devil runs the world system at the present time? God wants us to know that the spirit realm is active in world affairs (Daniel 10:12–13).

Yes, our Heavenly Father has his hands on the wheel of the bus as he guides it to the destination of his planning. But during the ride, there is a bad dude playing the role of Program Coordinator. He is wily and deceptive. And because he is the prince of the power of the air, we should expect treachery and deception in world history.

So, is this chapter about encouraging people to become more suspicious and paranoid? Not really. It's about understanding the nature of the age we live in and who is behind so much of the thought and decision-making in the modern world. It's about recognizing the unseen spiritual warfare that is a part of our seen world. It's about acknowledging and being aware of our spiritual enemy who is bent on deceiving us and dragging us all to hell with him if he could.

To think like God recognizes Satan as playing a bigger role in this world than is visible to the naked eye. It also involves a cautionary approach to official explanations, recognizing that evil motives are part and parcel of this world system. But it also involves a remembrance that those who walk with God will eventually win, even if they get hurt by satanically inspired human conspiracies along the way.

The Apostle John reminds us about the final destination for the great deceiver himself. He may be having a field day now, but in the end, he is doomed. *"Then the devil, who had deceived them, was thrown into the fiery lake of burning sulfur, joining the beast and the false prophet. There they will be tormented day and night forever and ever"* (Revelation 20:10).

DISCUSSION QUESTIONS

1. How do the average citizen and the scientific community view conspiracy theories differently?

2. What are the basic tenets of conspiracy theory?

3. What phrases does the Bible use to describe Satan and how do these relate to our perception of conspiracy theory?

4. Give some examples of conspiracies that were masterminded in the biblical narrative.

5. What grand conspiracy is Satan scheming for the end times?

6. What organizations might conceivably play a role in that plan (#5)?

7. Is there any proof that significant conspiracies have actually been executed in history?

8. Should a Christian lean more towards or against conspiracy theories? Why?

Chapter 11

"I like to ask a lot of questions."

"Where are you?"

~ Genesis 3:9

It is common to think of the Bible as a book of answers. In reality, it should also be recognized as a collection of questions that God asks in an attempt to challenge and change our thinking. Scripture is replete with commands and positive encouragements. But there are also an abundance of questions that God has for us to consider.

Humans ask questions for a variety of reasons. Sometimes we are looking for an answer to a matter that we do not understand. Sometimes we are trying to solve a problem. We may pose a query because we are honestly searching for the truth. Sometimes we even ask questions to confirm our unbelief. Have you ever heard someone ask, "How can a loving God allow so much evil in the world?"

On the contrary, God asks questions for very different reasons. Primarily, the Creator desires relationship with his Creation. God asks questions first and foremost to establish and maintain communion and communication with us. Where we will ask questions to find things out, perhaps to benefit ourselves, God asks questions in order to invite us into an intimate dialogue with him so that we might be changed.

And the more we are changed into thinking like God thinks, the more we realize that it's all about relationship. The

Bible is not just a book telling us stuff we need to know, it's also a record of the Lord of the Universe pursuing an ongoing conversation, causing us to self-examine and self-reflect, encouraging us to scrutinize our inner being.

God does not do or say useless things. Consequently, his questions must be taken seriously and answered honestly. That is the whole point. For the answers we give to God's questions often become defining moments in our spiritual journey. Not only do they reveal what is important to him, our answers reveal what is truly important to us.

It started in the garden. *"Where are you?"* God asked the disobedient couple (Genesis 3:9). Right from the start we see God asks a lot of questions with double meaning. Yes, they were hiding, but I'm pretty sure God knew their physical location. Was he not probing, "Adam and Eve, where are you—spiritually?" *"'Who told you that you were naked?' the Lord God asked. 'Have you eaten from the tree whose fruit I commanded you not to eat?'"* (Genesis 3:11) *"What have you done?"* he asked Eve (Genesis 3:13).

God asked these questions when he already knew the answers. Why? Instead of directly hammering the newlyweds for their disobedience, God wanted the sinners themselves to talk about what just happened. His questions assigned blame, but also gave Adam and Eve the opportunity to accept responsibility for their actions. Through questions, God provided the couple with space to reflect on the events and gain perspective on the reality of their sin. This is one way that God helps humans experience true repentance. Since repentance is a change of mind, there must be thought involved for it to be genuine. What better way to get the brain thinking than to ask it a question?

"Why are you so angry?" the Lord asked the next generation sinner (Genesis 4:6). Cain's offering was not accepted by the Lord because of a deliberate act of disobedience. God assured him, *"You will be accepted if you do what is right"* (Genesis 4:7). Cain was dejected because the

work of his hands was not what God desired. The Lord wanted obedience and so he questioned the young man about why he was so full of rage. We probably do the same thing today. We knowingly disobey God and then get upset with the consequences. It seems apparent that God will, on occasion, ask us questions to wake us up from the silliness of our rebellion which is so plain to everyone but ourselves.

After Abel's murder, the Lord asked Cain, *"Where is your brother?"* (Genesis 4:9) Cain responded with a lie followed by a cheeky return question: *"Am I my brother's guardian?"* (Genesis 4:9) When God asks us a question, it's probably not a good idea to respond with a disrespectful counter-question. God asks us tough questions to get us to face situations truthfully. Lying comes so naturally to us; we need God's questions to assist us in facing reality. Just as God asked Eve, he repeated to Cain: *"What have you done?"* (Genesis 4:10)

Even today, we need these questions asked of ourselves on a regular basis. Where am I? Where am I in my relationship with the Lord? What have I done? Do I understand the depth and ramifications of my sin? Why am I so angry because the Lord is asking me to do the right thing?

Moving chronologically through the biblical narrative, the next batch of great questions from God is found in the story of Job. The Book of Job is bursting with questions—human questions for God mostly, but splendidly awesome God-questions for man in chapters 38–41. After the humans all had their chance to speak and had contributed their best theology to understanding Job's suffering, God weighed in.

"Where were you when I laid the foundations of the earth?" he began (Job 38:4). The tide of challenges to human wisdom and power continued: *"Have you ever commanded the morning to appear and caused the dawn to rise in the east?"* (Job 38:12) *"Do you know the laws of the universe? Can you use them to regulate the earth?"* (Job 38:33) Dozens

and dozens of challenging questions spilled out until the glory of God outshone the puniness of man.

When the onslaught was complete, Job broke out into repentance, and confessed that in comparison to the wisdom and majesty of the Creator, his experiences and opinions did not mean much:

> *You asked, 'Who is this that questions my wisdom with such ignorance?' It is I—and I was talking about things I knew nothing about, things far too wonderful for me. You said, 'Listen and I will speak! I have some questions for you, and you must answer them.' I had only heard about you before, but now I have seen you with my own eyes. I take back everything I said, and I sit in dust and ashes to show my repentance* (Job 42:3–6).

Sometimes God asks us questions to expose our limitations as humans and give us a glimpse of his marvelous glory. Job's contrition is a model of how to respond properly to such a situation. He understood the significance of the questions God asked him. Job knew he could not answer them but he also knew why they needed to be asked. Job's transformation came not from answers, but from the questions themselves and his appropriate humility beneath those questions.

And there can be great consolation in this line of questioning. If we listen carefully, we gain great comfort and assurance of God's sovereignty by hearing him ask questions that only he can answer. At times, evil people prevail. But in due time, justice will come. Nothing can thwart God's retribution. In his judgment of Edom, a wicked country neighboring Israel, he said, *"For who is like me, and who can challenge me? What ruler can oppose my will?"* (Jeremiah 49:19) These, of course, are rhetorical questions. But as we hear the Lord ask them, we are assured that he's in control of all things, all the time.

God's sovereignty was evident in the stories of the Jewish patriarchs, but he also had questions for them to bring about transformations in their thinking. When the Lord gave Abraham the news of Isaac's upcoming birth, his 89-year-old wife scoffed inside. *"Then the Lord said to Abraham, 'Why did Sarah laugh? Why did she say, 'Can an old woman like me have a baby?' Is anything too hard for the Lord? I will return about this time next year, and Sarah will have a son'"* (Genesis 18:13–14). God wanted the father of his chosen nation to understand that there is nothing funny about his divine plans. He also wanted him to comprehend that as long as God is in the story, nothing is impossible. These truths need to grip our hearts today.

As does the fact that encounters with God change our lives. Jacob learned this the night he wrestled with the Lord and came out with a dislocated hip. At this watershed moment in his life—the night before he was to meet his embittered brother (Genesis 27:41)—Jacob left the encounter a new man. Although the full significance of this Genesis 32 account is difficult to understand, the question God asked in the middle of the match is powerful. *"'What is your name?' the man asked. He replied, 'Jacob.' 'Your name will no longer be Jacob,' the man told him. 'From now on you will be called Israel, because you have fought with God and with men and have won'"* (Genesis 32:27–28).

When the Lord asked Jacob to say his name out loud, he was calling for him to confess his sinful nature. Jacob (heel-grabber or supplanter) now became Israel (one who has prevailed with God). Until this point, Jacob had got his way with Esau through blackmail and deception. Now he would face his brother and the rest of his life with the knowledge that he was a man touched by God. Even today, there may be value in our public confession of who we are naturally without Christ, followed by a recognition of who we have become since being touched by God.

On other occasions, God asks questions to get his followers back on track when they wander away. Right after the prophet Elijah experienced a huge emotional high on Mount Carmel (1 Kings 18), he succumbed to a deep depression because of Jezebel's death threat (1 Kings 19:3–4). He ended up fleeing to a cave where the Lord had a piercing question for him:

> *"What are you doing here, Elijah?" Elijah replied, "I have zealously served the Lord God Almighty. But the people of Israel have broken their covenant with you, torn down your altars, and killed every one of your prophets. I am the only one left, and now they are trying to kill me, too"* (1 Kings 19:9–10).

After showing Elijah three miraculous signs of cataclysmic proportions, God repeated his initial question. Elijah gave the same reply. In response to Elijah's pouting, God challenged him to put things into perspective. He gave him something to think about. "In light of all I have done through you by my mighty power, why are you hiding on the sidelines, feeling sorry for yourself like you are the only one in the world oppressed for doing good?" God's response was both an encouragement and an exhortation:

> *Go back the same way you came, and travel to the wilderness of Damascus. When you arrive there, anoint Hazael to be king of Aram. Then anoint Jehu son of Nimshi to be king of Israel, and anoint Elisha son of Shaphat from the town of Abel-meholah to replace you as my prophet. Anyone who escapes from Hazael will be killed by Jehu, and those who escape Jehu will be killed by Elisha! Yet I will preserve 7,000 others in Israel who have never bowed down to Baal or kissed him!* (1 Kings 19:15–18)

God still had work for Elijah to do (three positional anointings), and, contrary to his emotions, he was not the only true follower of Jehovah left in the land. God was working in the hearts of thousands of others. Sometimes we need the same kick in the pants. "What are you doing here?" When there is work to be done and righteous living to be lived, get busy. Quit feeling sorry for yourself. Stop hiding in your cave like a pathetic loser.

In contrast to Elijah's self-centered moping, the Lord of the Universe would like to hear more responses like the one Isaiah gave during his heavenly vision: *"Then I heard the Lord asking, 'Whom should I send as a messenger to this people? Who will go for us?' I said, 'Here I am. Send me'"* (Isaiah 6:8).

The pattern is quite common. God asks us questions to challenge our thinking and expose our wills. He wants to bring out the best in us by making us respond to his probing inquiries. According to Phyllis A. Cooper, "There are more than three hundred questions attributed to God in the Hebrew scriptures."[20] And the pattern continues in earnest in the New Testament. Jesus was the ultimate inquisitor.

At the age of twelve, he asked his panicked parents who thought they had lost him at the Passover, *"Didn't you know that I must be in my Father's house?"* (Luke 2:49) Even in pre-adolescence, the Messiah preferred questions to answers. Mary and Joseph's response was human and typical: *"But they didn't understand what he meant"* (Luke 2:50). Often we don't fully understand what Jesus meant by his questions either, but there is great merit in pondering them.

"What do you want?" he asked some disciples who started following him (John 1:38). People who tag along with Jesus have many different motives.

"Where are your accusers?" he asked the woman caught in adultery (John 8:10). When Jesus forgives us, is there anyone who can condemn us?

"But who do you say that I am?" he asked his disciples in response to the various public opinions of the day (Luke 9:20).

---

[20] Cited April 17, 2010 at http://www.rosedogbookstore.com/ qugodasinhes.html

The world has many confused notions about Christ. Our view of him entirely affects our behavior and our destiny.

"If you love only those who love you, why should you get credit for that?" he challenged the crowds (Luke 6:32). Jesus wanted us to know that he and his Heavenly Father's standards are always higher than ours. Thinking merely like a human leads us to believe we're doing better than we really are.

"Why are you afraid?" he asked his sea-soaked companions in the midst of the storm (Matthew 8:26). *"Where is your faith?"* (Luke 8:25) Is there really any circumstance or problem that is bigger than the Creator of the Universe? Could the maker of the molecules of the sea not also command its destiny with ease? Based on what we've seen of God's goodness and power and faithfulness in the past, can we not believe in him for our troubles today?

"Would you like to get well?" he asked the sick man in Jerusalem who had been bed-ridden for thirty-eight years (John 5:6). Being well implies a whole new level of responsibility. The sick man had everything done for him. Health would mean a fresh degree of duty and accountability. Do we really want everything Jesus has for us? Do we really want to deal with our sin or do we love it so much we would rather stay put and not have the obligation of faithfulness?

"Who touched me?" he asked the crowd when the woman with a twelve year hemorrhage fingered the fringe of his robe (Luke 8:44–45). Many people reach out in faith to Christ, but it appears that the Messiah wants us to make our faith public. When his power transforms us into new creatures, he wants us to let others know about it.

"Where are the other nine?" he asked the Samaritan leper whom he had cleansed (Luke 17:17). God constantly gives good gifts. Only about ten percent take notice and offer the appropriate thanksgiving and praise. Full and complete healing comes only with true gratitude.

"What do you want me to do for you?" he asked blind Bartimaeus outside the city of Jericho (Mark 10:51). Bartimaeus' obvious response was the restoration of his sight, but it was his proclamation in faith that made him well (Mark 10:52). I wonder how often we fail to get what we need because we neglect to ask in faith, or even ask at all. We're good at fretting and stewing, but not so good at faith.

"Who is my mother? Who are my brothers?" he asked the crowd in response to his family's desire to have a private word with him (Matthew 12:48). Jesus answered this one himself— only those individuals who obediently do the will of God are considered to be his true family. Heavenly entrance and reward have nothing to do with earthly family relationships.

"Now which of these three would you say was a neighbor?" he asked those who listened to the parable of the Good Samaritan (Luke 10:36). The crowd replied that the true neighbor was the one who showed mercy, even though he was a social outcast. How often do those in positions of power and prestige fail to show mercy to the needy? What would it look like for us to be true neighbors in our neighborhoods today?

"What were you discussing out on the road?" he asked his disciples after they secretly argued about who was the greatest among them (Mark 9:33). How embarrassing for the Lord to expose some of the things we talk about—whether selfish, lewd, or prideful. But do not our quiet thoughts and comments reveal the true nature of our hearts and level of commitment? And do we not realize that he hears everything we say?

"Do you think I have come to bring peace to the earth?" he asked his disciples (Luke 12:51). Jesus is not a warmonger, but following him in this fallen world does not guarantee a Shangri-La outcome. When we expose, challenge, or try to deal with the sin in our lives and in our communities, there is tension and conflict. Following Jesus involves questions and commitments that storm the very gates of hell. The devil will

not go down without a fight, and that fight can spread even into family relationships.

"Are you also going to leave?" he asked his disciples in the face of a mass desertion by many of their colleagues (John 6:67). What would it take for us to abandon the Savior? Will others falling away cause us to lose heart also? Maybe some of us have left and we haven't even realized it yet.

"Do you love me?" he asked Peter after his resurrection (John 21:17). He still asks us this question every day. Do you love me more than your desires? Do you love me more than your plans? Do you love me more than your dreams? Or do you love your sin more than anything else?

"Are you able to drink from the bitter cup of suffering I am about to drink?" he asked James and John in response to their request to have special places in the Kingdom of God (Matthew 20:22). Are we ready to suffer for our identification with Christ? The Scriptures promise persecution for those willing to live a godly life for the Savior.

And the list goes on—*"Why can't you understand what I am saying?"* (John 8:43) *"Which of you can truthfully accuse me of sin?"* (John 8:46) *"Why don't you believe me?"* (John 8:46) *"Would you betray the Son of Man with a kiss?"* (Luke 22:48)

Three of the last questions the Lord (or his angels) asked his friends were quite meaningful. *"Why are you sleeping?"* (Luke 22:46) *"Why are you crying?"* (John 20:15) *"Why are you standing here staring into heaven?"* (Acts 1:11) These questions summarize our all too frequent position in response to the Lord. So often we're doing the wrong thing at the wrong time. Instead of praying, we're sleeping. Instead of rejoicing, we're weeping. And, instead of getting busy with Kingdom work, we stand there gazing into the sky.

Perhaps if we more regularly heeded Christ's condemnatory query, *"Haven't you read the scriptures?"* (Matthew 19:4), we would find ourselves doing the right things more often. Jesus continually corrected poor thinking around him by plainly reminding his listeners that much of their confusion could be corrected by simply reading the Scriptures.

For it is in the reading of the Scriptures that we learn that God has a lot of useful questions for us to consider. From Adam and Eve in the Garden to the rich young ruler in Judea to us today, the Lord engages individuals with arresting precision and brings to light faulty thinking about ourselves and our Creator. These questions are as penetrating today as they were thousands of years ago. Through them our minds can be renovated as we gain a deeper understanding of the truth about his divine nature and our condition.

Typically, we spend a lot of time asking God questions. Perhaps we should spend more time attempting to answer the ones he has asked us.

DISCUSSION QUESTIONS

1. How should we view the Bible in terms of its purpose for our lives?

2. Why does God ask us questions? Does he always expect an answer?

3. How might some of God's questions for us have a double meaning?

4. God asked Job a lot of questions. What was the Lord communicating to him?

5. "What are you doing here Elijah?" What was God doing in the prophet's life with this line of questioning?

6. "Jesus was the ultimate inquisitor." Explain.

7. Explain the significance of any three questions asked by Jesus.

8. What do you think of the concept articulated in the last paragraph of this chapter?

Chapter 12

"Dads are awesome too."

"Fathers, don't exasperate your children...Take them by the hand and lead them in the way of the Master."

~ Ephesians 6:4 MSG

If aliens peered down on our planet from outer space and tuned into our satellite TV signals, they would probably come to at least one certain conclusion about the human race—that men are idiots.

Even though our political and economic spheres are still largely tipped in favor of the male species, the marketing media in the social arena portray men as buffoons. In cold medicine commercials, Dad is completely helpless while Mom is the superhero who comes to rescue her family from all viral and bacterial assaults. In advertisements for new vehicles, Mom alone possesses the fiscal savvy and good judgment needed to pick the appropriate SUV for the brood.

I realize that marketing tactics are based on the fact that women make most of the consumer purchases in our culture, but this misandric trend has gotten a little out of hand. Perhaps as a pendulum swing in reaction to the extreme abuse women have experienced historically, men take a disproportionate beating in the media about their overall ineptitude.

Judging by the sheer volume of male-mocking in advertising, I think it is reasonable to conclude that human thinking has a tendency to downplay the important role of fathers. Male behavior in general has not helped our cause either. Recent trends towards the absentee father are shocking. "Unbelievable as it seems, more than half of the world's children are estimated to spend at least part of their childhood without a father in the home. Never before have so many men abandoned their wives and children."[21]

Western thinking has a muddled philosophical mix regarding paternity. On the one hand, men are told that they are useless around the home. Because they are of little value to the kids, dads are subtly allowed to abdicate their domestic duties in order to pursue other endeavors, whether that be tailgating with the buddies at the football game or an all-consuming claw up the corporate ladder. On the other hand, because of our general poor track record, there is this ever-present aura of shame hovering over every father's head associated with falling short of expectations.

In the mind of God, however, both father-bashing and father-absenteeism are foreign concepts. Right from the start, God intended men to fulfill a high and worthy calling within the family structure alongside their wives. Do women deserve full adoration for all their faithful and sacrificial nurturing? Of course. Mothers are great. But in the mind of God, dads are awesome too.

I am troubled to see this father-bashing prevalent even within church culture. I have no scientific proof for this theory, but this is what I have noticed over the years. Most Mother's Day sermons are tremendously encouraging pep rallies with one common theme: "Moms, you are wonderful!" The pastor waxes eloquently about the greatness of moms, describing the fantastic job they have done in raising all the impish children of the world. The intent of the service is to leave moms and all family members feeling warm and fuzzy.

In contrast, Father's Day sermons seem a bit more...preachy. The assumption is that dads are messing up

[21] Cited Feb 16, 2009 http://oldarchive.godspy.com/reviews/In-Praise-of-Fatherhood-by-Johann-Christoph-Arnold.cfm.html

and the cure is a good homiletic kick in the pants. Fathers are warned against potential failure while mothers are praised for success. Sometimes this message is delivered in a fairly delicate manner, but the memo is still clear: "Dads, you are falling short. You need to pull up your socks and do better."

When was the last time you ever heard a preacher scold the ladies in the middle of a Mother's Day sermon, telling them that they had better smarten up? I know for certain that I have been bawled out a few times on the third Sunday of June. I fear to estimate how many men have left a Father's Day service feeling guilty as opposed to feeling warm and fuzzy.

Sometimes churches give mothers a gift at the end of the service on their special day—a flower or plant of some sort. This is a nice idea. But most of the gifts given to dads on Father's Day are of the didactic nature. Perhaps it's a little book or pamphlet on improved fathering, or, the classic, a small rolled-up scroll with some wise words on how to do it better—'The Ten Commandments of Fatherhood' for instance.

Moms get flowers; dads get literature. "Hey moms, here's a pretty gift for you because we love you. You're awesome!" "Hey dads, you suck! Here's some stuff to read. Try to get it right next time."

Agreed—mothers deserve all the accolades and adulation they can get, especially moms who have survived or are presently surviving a wayward child, or those who are courageously forging a family life without a husband. Moms, your hearts are full of love and you put up with far more than you deserve in the nurturing of your children, but dads are awesome too.

God's thoughts on fathering are unambiguous. He wants men to be strong loving leaders in their homes and he has left us many clear directives on how to be a great dad. The first instruction appeared in the Pentateuch:

> *And you must love the Lord your God with all your heart, all your soul, and all your strength. And you must commit yourselves wholeheartedly to these commands that I am*

giving you today. Repeat them again and again to your children. Talk about them when you are at home and when you are on the road, when you are going to bed and when you are getting up (Deuteronomy 6:5–7).

God desires fathers to be present in the lives of their children, teaching them so naturally the truths of God throughout the day, no one would even notice there was a sermon going on. Solomon's exhortation to *"Train up a child in the way he should go"* (Proverbs 22:6 NASB) obviously involves both Mom and Dad, but fathers are given the primary instructive role in the familial structure. Solomon's own father had taught him to *"get wisdom"* and *"develop good judgment"* (Proverbs 4:5). Yes, good fathers should give their kids *"good gifts"* (Matthew 7:11) and try to leave an inheritance to their off-spring (Proverbs 13:22), but their principal role is teaching, by word and by example.

Sometimes this teaching takes the form of loving correction. Children should learn divine truths through their father's discipline. *"For the Lord corrects those he loves, just as a father corrects a child in whom he delights"* (Proverbs 3:12). Sometimes this teaching involves persistent petitioning. *"And you know that we treated each of you as a father treats his own children. We pleaded with you, encouraged you, and urged you to live your lives in a way that God would consider worthy"* (1 Thessalonians 2:11–12).

Of course, the instruction only has meaning and blessing when the teacher is living a life of integrity (Proverbs 20:7). In God's sovereign economy, a father's sins can impact a child's future (2 Kings 5:27). And, unsurprisingly, the blessings and curses that flow out of a father's mouth can have an extraordinary impact on the course of a child's life.

Using the Scriptures as a basis for all teaching and correction of children (2 Timothy 3:16), fathers are to *"bring them up with the discipline and instruction that comes from the Lord"* (Ephesians 6:4). But this verse also says, *"Fathers, do not provoke your children to anger by the way you treat them."*

The command is interesting—"Dads, stop unnecessarily ticking off your kids by being a jerk." Yes, you have the authority to be in charge, but how are you using this power?

Bad fathering exasperates children. It makes them angry and loads them up with baggage they will struggle to unpack throughout their lives. Bad fathering takes many forms—unreasonable severity, unpredictable injustice, cruel demands, needless restrictions, selfish insistence, and dictatorial authority. These behaviors suck the life out of a child—they kill her affection and make him feel unworthy of Dad's love.

At first glance, it seems like it should be easy. Little children come into the world so hungry for the attention of a man they can trust and admire. But sin, selfishness, and a system of worldliness morally disqualify a number of men, rendering them unable to *"manage [their] children and household[s] well"* (1 Timothy 3:12).

But thinking like God on the subject of fatherhood involves far more than simply reinforcing the standard list of admonitions; it also involves a celebration of the good things many fathers *are* doing already, particularly those demonstrations of love that are uniquely masculine.

Sure, men are easy targets and some fathers do need a little boot in the behind. The list of crimes is frighteningly renowned—abusive, emotionally distant, intimately disengaged, and generally missing in action. It's not hard to find an example of a dad who has messed up.

But instead of dwelling solely on the negative, we need to commemorate the positive loving behaviors frequently exhibited by many fathers today. Whether or not they recognize it themselves, countless dads are loving and leading their families in ways that moms would find difficult to do on their own. And for such success stories, these fathers deserve to be honored.

Good fathering entails many different facets of love, but let's consider three particular ones that are distinctively mannish and worthy of admiration—protection, provision, and pushing.

Fathers have the unique ability to protect their families. Generally speaking, there is vulnerability in youth and in the female gender, and fathers have the strength to make the home a safe place. How many men send their wives downstairs in the middle of the night to check out that big clunk? Who goes outside to investigate or intercept what might be a potential act of vandalism or destruction of property? Fathers make the home safe and create an atmosphere of security that provides the family with a peace of mind that is often missing when Dad is not there.

Once the children start to come of age, most dads display a natural ability to protect their precious little daughters from all those ogling eyes that start to appear, those little critters that need about ten more years to mature. Sometimes a look is all that's required for the young man to get the picture; sometimes a comment involving the words 'gun' or 'corpse' is necessary for him to get the hint.

But good dads also know how to look after their sons, to shield them from themselves and their human nature, to watch out for them as they mature. They also guard their sons from hidden dangers. The warm love of a father can help young men turn into great future fathers themselves, as they are protected from the fears of leadership and intimacy.

When fathers lovingly provide protection for their families in these ways, they glorify God by acting just like him. For our Heavenly Father also lovingly protects us from harm. The Psalmist wrote: *"He will cover you with his feathers. He will shelter you with his wings. His faithful promises are your armor and protection"* (Psalm 91:4).

God protects his spiritual family, enabling us to rest securely in his love. He even protects us from situations that we are not yet able to handle. The Apostle Paul gave an example of this in 1 Corinthians 10:13. *"The temptations in your life are no different from what others experience. And*

God is faithful. He will not allow the temptation to be more than you can stand. When you are tempted, he will show you a way out so that you can endure."

God the Father knows just what we can handle, just like earthly fathers know what their kids can handle. He protects us from those situations that would completely wipe us out. He takes care of us just like an earthly father guards his children against situations that are too much for them.

Like God, good fathers protect their families, but they also provide for their families in a number of loving ways. Granted, twenty-first century mothers now assist fathers in the provision of food, shelter, and clothing. But Dad's provision supersedes these basics.

You see, fatherly provision transcends money. Dads are equipped to provide a special brand of leadership in the home, a leadership that involves making tough decisions, solving family problems in a reasonable fashion, repairing cars, managing home repairs and renovations, and even planning family vacations.

A father also has the ability to provide wise counsel from his wide range of experience. Often he can give a sense of stability to potentially volatile situations by balancing off a holistic, emotional perspective with a focused analysis that stems from a highly compartmentalized masculine brain.

Fathers supply a plethora of provisions for their families in the same way that our Heavenly Father provides for us, his spiritual children. It's easy for us to take God's provision for granted, just like we take our earthly fathers for granted. Even when no one notices, dads quietly take care of a lot of uncomfortable responsibilities, like scraping the car windows in the winter, or aerating the lawn in the summer.

God the Father watches over us, protecting us, giving us what we need; but he also pushes us on to higher levels. In the same manner, earthly fathers lovingly push their children on to higher levels. This role is tricky though. It is a common complaint—"Dad was never satisfied with anything I did."

The story is usually told with the father as the villain—the hard, insensitive brute who destroys the spirit of the child because of perpetual criticism or perennial dissatisfaction.

But if we fathers faithfully imitate our Heavenly Father, we cannot avoid the task of pushing. It is part of the father's role to press his kids on to their full potential. Dad sees ability and instinctively challenges his kids to strive higher, to not be content with just getting by. Where Mom sees danger, Dad sees possibilities. Mom says, "Get down out of that tree, you'll get hurt." Dad proudly says, "Did you see how high Jr. climbed today?"

Dad will comment on the number of goals scored by the budding young hockey star, while Mom will be concerned that little Gretzky may catch his death of pneumonia by being out on the rink too long. I wonder how far Wayne Gretzky would have gone without the drive of his father, pushing him to be the best he could be?

Why do you suppose that a father's all-time favorite sport is wrestling with his kids? We like to push them on, to make them stronger. We eagerly anticipate the day when our sons will be able to take us down—a day long past in my case.

Dads love to envision greater, more challenging futures for their children. Like a hen, a mother's natural inclination is to keep her chicks close to her where they can be nurtured; but fathers push their kids towards autonomy. When the first child leaves home, mothers weep while fathers burst with pride because of their offspring's independence.

Dads see the value of their children experiencing hardships because they know it will equip them for the future. Fathers demonstrate their love for their children by preparing them to face life on their own, with the ability to run their own families. Fathers allow trials because they believe in their kids. They trust them to be able to survive and to come out the other end stronger.

And so it is with God. He believes in us. He sees our potential in Christ, and says, just like an earthly father, "You

can do it, my boy! You can do it, my girl! I believe in you."
When we make insufficient progress, he's not content. His
Holy Spirit hounds us and coaxes us to greater holiness. He
allows us to undergo trials because he knows they make us
stronger. And when we need discipline, he takes care of that
too.

God is obviously the perfect father and we strive to
imitate him. But you fathers, sitting with this book in your
hands, are doing a lot of good things, things that deserve
honor. This is not a provocation to feel guilty or depressed
about your failures and shortcomings. This is not an occasion
to feel overwhelmingly discouraged and to give up. This is a
time to thank God for the skill and opportunity he has given
you as a father. It's also an opportunity for all of us to bless
our own fathers and appreciate them for the contribution they
have made to our lives, despite their inadequacies. It's a time
to forgive our fathers for their transgressions against us. It's a
time to honor our fathers for all they have deposited into our
lives through their protection, provision, and pushing.

Some dads are incredible. Some are average. Some are
awful. Some of you have a father you wish you didn't have.
There is no easy answer to your pain and disappointment. But
there is always hope in the love of God and there is always
optimism for a better future, one where a new generation
breaks the cycle of sin and neglect by fully embracing the role
of fatherhood as God intended it to be—active, involved, and
fully integrated with an obedient and living faith.

And I believe the next generation of fathers will be better
trained by encouragement than by guilt. You are not a
buffoon. But you must not abandon your high and noble
calling. Fathers, keep up the great work of protecting,
providing for, and pushing your children onward. You are
mimicking God through these efforts.

Coach your sons to be good fathers also. Properly trained
fathers will influence and change the lives of countless people,
because true fatherhood does not just mean being a father to

your own children. We can also be fathers to many other children around us, especially those who grow up in single-parent homes, or those whose fathers are in some way absent. In this manner, we not only enjoy the blessings of a God-ordained family life, but also have the chance to become the hands and feet of a God who is a Father to the fatherless.

Moms are great, that's a given. But in God's thinking, dads are awesome too.

DISCUSSION QUESTIONS

1. What mixed message do our media portray about fathers and men in general?

2. What is the difference between many Mother's Day and Father's Day church services?

3. Describe the divine model for proper fatherhood.

4. What are some of the ways fathers exasperate their children?

5. What three facets of a father's love are uniquely masculine?

6. How do these behaviors (#5) resemble the way God the Father loves his children?

7. How does one overcome the baggage of bad fathering?

8. How can godly fathers fulfill their divine role beyond their own families?

Chapter 13

"I do look at the heart, but I also appreciate a well-trained mind and body."

"God owns the whole works. So let people see God in and through your body."

~ 1 Corinthians 6:20 MSG

At fifty, my body is becoming less attractive. The face looks a little fuller and the belly increasingly portly, seemingly beyond repair. I still play hockey once a week, but there is not enough physical activity in the other six days to restore my figure back to its taut early twenties form. Rather than taking steps to address the issue, I am tempted to quote 1 Samuel 16:7, *"People judge by outward appearance, but the Lord looks at the heart."*

But instead of proof-texting for our own benefit, we need to think more deeply about God's view of the total human package. Left alone, it's easy for us to think one-dimensionally. The soul that cares little for the Savior may focus solely on outward appearance. The saved saint, on the way to Heaven, may neglect the rigors necessary to realize remarkable human accomplishment. Both perspectives are incomplete on their own.

Truly, God has placed within us incredible potential for achievement in agriculture, architecture, the arts, athletics, business, economics, engineering, literature, medicine, and science. The Almighty has given us the ability to become great in many fields of earthly endeavor.

Without a spiritual awakening, many people spend their time on Earth with a single purpose—to achieve something worthwhile or momentous either with their minds or their bodies. Some become wholly devoted to their careers, hoping to achieve the highest level of promotion attainable. Others live in the gym, totally obsessed with the shape of their sculptured torsos. Some devote every spare minute to becoming virtuosos in their musical fields, while others chase Forex transactions around the clock to amass large fortunes. Lacking a connection with the Creator, the unsaved can easily remain focused on outward attainment, neglecting matters of the heart.

However, it is also easy for Christians to be guilty of a similar one-dimensional focus, thinking only of heart matters to the neglect of notable outward achievements. Once we have experienced salvation in Christ, we may be fooled into thinking that many earthly endeavors are now pointless. For the born again believer, devoting large amounts of time to things that will one day burn seems to be an act of futility. After all, doesn't God tell us to think only about Heaven? The Apostle Paul wrote:

> *Since you have been raised to new life with Christ, set your sights on the realities of heaven, where Christ sits in the place of honor at God's right hand. Think about the things of heaven, not the things of earth. For you died to this life, and your real life is hidden with Christ in God* (Colossians 3:1–3).

Such a text by itself leaves the impression that all worldly work is meaningless. But if we read further in the same passage, we realize this is not true. Paul also says, *"Whatever you do, do your work heartily, as for the Lord rather than for men"* (Colossians 3:23 NASB). We must be careful not to cherry pick Scriptures, making the Bible say only what we want it to say. As we examine the whole counsel of God, we notice the Lord's view is far more balanced than ours, focusing both on outer achievement and inner character. To think like God about the duty of man on Earth is to hold both inner heart matters and outer accomplishments in high esteem. God is saying, "I do look at the heart, but I also appreciate a well-trained mind and body."

That God cares deeply about the heart is a given. But right from the beginning, he also instructed man to perform useful work with his hands. *"Be fruitful and multiply, and fill the earth, and subdue it"* he told Adam and Eve. *"Rule over the fish of the sea and over the birds of the sky and over every living thing that moves on the earth"* (Genesis 1:28 NASB). That sounds like a big job. No lollygagging in the garden for the newlyweds. It was God's intention from the start that mankind's behavior should reflect the Lord's constructive and creative nature. Early in the narrative, ancestors of the first couple began to create innovative technologies—tent-making (Genesis 4:20), musical instrument inventions (Genesis 4:21), bronze and iron forging (Genesis 4:22).

God's command for Noah to build a 450–foot long ship was a colossal engineering feat. Noah must have been a master craftsman to be able to construct such an ocean-going vessel five millennia ago. This massive structure was designed to house hundreds, if not thousands, of animals while weathering a torrential marine storm. Its production was a great human achievement. But, it was also part of a divine plan. That's what makes this story absorbing. For in it, we see man's courageous labors working hand in hand with God's purposes. The ark was a fantastic building venture completed by a man with a good heart. *"Noah was a righteous man, the only blameless person living on earth at the time, and he walked in close fellowship with God"* (Genesis 6:9).

The Tower of Babel, on the other hand, is a prime example of a monstrous building project attempted by people with bad hearts. *"Then they said, 'Come, let's build a great city for ourselves with a tower that reaches into the sky. This will make us famous and keep us from being scattered all over the world'"* (Genesis 11:4). Instead of obeying the Lord's command to fill the Earth, this early group of humans wanted to stick together and build a huge tower for their own purposes—to reach high into the heavens and establish a great name for themselves. Obviously, the required technological skill and architectural knowledge for Babel must have been gargantuan. But no matter how great the physical exploit, if it's done with selfish intent, it is worthless and will eventually come to ruin.

Historical ruins are pregnant with pointed examples of humans devoting immeasurable resources to gigantic schemes built solely for human glorification rather than God's purposes—the Great Pyramids, Nebuchadnezzar's Babylon, China's Great Wall, the Incas' Machu Picchu. Like the Tower of Babel, these and other such overwhelming human achievements were about arrogance, protection of assets, and bragging rights. They had nothing to do with the plans of God, submission to his will, or the enhancement of personal holiness.

But just because some people do it wrong does not eliminate the fact that God is still interested in notable human efforts of personal and societal augmentation, especially when those efforts are related to the work of God in his Kingdom. Throughout the Old Testament, when God was at work in lives or in building ventures, there was always a sense of excellence expected.

Was it just a coincidence that the Lord picked Moses to lead his chosen people out of Egyptian captivity? I doubt it. Moses was a very learned man. He grew up in Pharaoh's court and received the finest education possible. After forty years of formal training and noble grooming, and forty more years of contemplative service herding sheep in the wilderness, Moses was prepared to play this significant role in redemptive history.

After the Exodus, the benefits of Moses' training were obvious. On Mount Sinai, God used him as a conduit to deliver the entire Jewish legal system. He had the wisdom to provide godly judgment in response to matters of dispute amongst the Children of Israel (Exodus 18:13–16). When his father-in-law warned Moses about potential burn-out from his dawn-till-dusk court sessions, Moses had the expertise to select capable men who acted as his surrogate judges, handling the smaller cases while he continued to address the hard ones (Exodus 18:17–27). When it came time to build the Tabernacle, Moses oversaw the intricate work of many skilled craftsmen who constructed a spectacular portable temple for worship in the wilderness.

Besides being a brilliant man of the law, a prophet, a writer, an overseer, and an administrator, Moses seems to have taken good care of his body. When he died at the age of 120, Moses was still healthy—*"he was as strong as ever"* (Deuteronomy 34:7). The concluding remarks about this man were glowing: *"There has never been another prophet in Israel like Moses"* (Deuteronomy 34:10). But he was also rich in character: *"Now Moses was very humble—more humble than any other person on earth"* (Numbers 12:3). In this man we see a prime example of a blend of godly character and human achievement. He was a talented guy who had prepared well in the early years of his life. He achieved great deeds worthy of pride, but always remained in proper submission to God.

As God directed the construction of the Tabernacle in the wilderness, the standards were high. It was important to have talented workmen playing key roles. When building a house for Yahweh, where his children would meet and worship him, nothing slipshod or mediocre would do. Experts in linen design, metal-working, and wood-carving were required. The project involved a lot of first class work—*"beautifully stitched garments"* (Exodus 31:10), *"special gemstones"* (Exodus 35:27), *"skillfully embroidered cherubim"* (Exodus 36:8), *"finely woven linen...exquisite designs"* (Exodus 36:37), *"decorated tops"*, and many things *"overlaid with gold"* (Exodus 36:38).

> *Then Moses told the people of Israel, "The Lord...has filled Bezalel with the Spirit of God, giving him great wisdom, ability, and expertise in all kinds of crafts. He is a master craftsman, expert in working with gold, silver, and bronze. He is skilled in engraving and mounting gemstones and in carving wood. He is a master at every craft. And the Lord has given both him and Oholiab son of Ahisamach, of the tribe of Dan, the ability to teach their skills to others. The Lord has given them special skills as engravers, designers, embroiderers in blue, purple, and scarlet thread on fine linen cloth, and weavers. They excel as craftsmen and as designers"* (Exodus 35:30–35).

> *Moreover, I have given special skill to all the gifted craftsmen so they can make all the things I have commanded you to make* (Exodus 31:6).

> *All the women who were skilled in sewing and spinning prepared blue, purple, and scarlet thread, and fine linen cloth. All the women who were willing used their skills to spin the goat hair into yarn* (Exodus 35:25–26).

Obviously, all gifting comes from the Creator, but this story indicates that God specially endowed some of these artisans with incredible skill for their designated tasks. But like any artist or craftsman, practice is required to hone those divinely bestowed abilities. Humans are not robots or marionettes that simply move at the beckon command of the Almighty. God gives aptitude, but we need to develop these capacities for his glory.

The same situation occurred with the construction of the Temple in Jerusalem. Solomon asked the Phoenician king to the north if he had any talent he could share for the project. King Hiram replied:

I am sending you a master craftsman named Huram-abi, who is extremely talented...He is skillful at making things from gold, silver, bronze, and iron, and he also works with stone and wood. He can work with purple, blue, and scarlet cloth and fine linen. He is also an engraver and can follow any design given to him. He will work with your craftsmen and those appointed by my lord David, your father (2 Chronicles 2:13–14).

Those who have studied ancient Middle East history know of the splendor of Solomon's Temple. It was a magnificent structure with beautifully embroidered curtains, decorated pillars, an altar, a 16 500 gallon basin, golden lampstands, chains, sacrificial utensils, and dueling angel figurines with fifteen-foot wingspans.

He paneled the main room of the Temple with cypress wood, overlaid it with fine gold, and decorated it with carvings of palm trees and chains. He decorated the walls of the Temple with beautiful jewels and with gold from the land of Parvaim. He overlaid the beams, thresholds, walls, and doors throughout the Temple with gold, and he carved figures of cherubim on the walls (2 Chronicles 3:5–7).

The Temple was constructed for the glory of the Lord and was a *"magnificent structure, famous and glorious throughout the world"* (1 Chronicles 22:5). When it came time for its consecration, the worship service was like none other.

And the Levites who were musicians...and all their sons and brothers were dressed in fine linen robes and stood at the east side of the altar playing cymbals, lyres, and harps. They were joined by 120 priests who were playing trumpets. The trumpeters and singers performed together in unison to praise and give thanks to the Lord...At that moment a thick cloud filled the Temple of the Lord. The priests could not

*continue their service because of the cloud, for the glorious
presence of the Lord filled the Temple of God* (2 Chronicles
5:11–14).

Breath-taking! Talented humans using their gifts to obey the
Lord, first completing and now dedicating this outstanding
building project—the Lord was pleased. He responded, *"I
have heard your prayer and have chosen this Temple as the
place for making sacrifices"* (2 Chronicles 7:12).

We must be careful not to turn our worship into a vanity
show, but the Lord wants things done well in his house. The
Psalmist says, *"Sing a new song of praise to him; play
skillfully on the harp, and sing with joy"* (Psalm 33:3). Psalm
150 exhorts us to praise the Lord with a conglomeration of
multiple instruments—horn, lyre, harp, tambourine, strings,
flutes, and cymbals—all accompanied by choreographed
dancing. This kind of performance demands a lot of
disciplined training.

God's children should never be reluctant to polish their
skills through practice. David's musical and combative abilities
were most likely developed through countless hours of
performance while shepherding his father's flocks. When the
servants in King Saul's court sought for a good musician to
soothe him amidst his demonic oppression, they chose David.
One of them said, *"One of Jesse's sons from Bethlehem is a
talented harp player. Not only that—he is a brave warrior, a
man of war, and has good judgment. He is also a fine-looking
young man, and the Lord is with him"* (1 Samuel 16:18). And I
don't think David's defeat of Goliath was just a lucky shot;
after all, he chose only five stones from the brook and there
were five giants in the land at that time (2 Samuel 21:16–22). In
the years that followed, David's well-prepared military prowess
became increasingly evident.

Daniel is another example of a godly man who developed
his extraordinary faculties, making himself ready for God's
work when the timing was right. He was identified as being
innately bright, but he studied hard and disciplined his body

appropriately, thereby increasing his stature and favor amidst several Babylonian and Persian kings.

Ezra was a righteous and regimented man, well-versed in the Torah, who was used by God to re-settle thousands of Jewish exiles back in the Promised Land after their years of captivity.

Nehemiah was a devout believer and able leader who humbly confessed his sins and sought God's favor before approaching King Artaxerxes about re-building the demolished wall around Jerusalem (Nehemiah 1). The Book of Nehemiah details his exceptional administrative capabilities as he brought the project to full fruition amidst much opposition.

Esther was naturally gorgeous, but she spent twelve months in a beautification program (Esther 2:12) so that she might win King Xerxes' favor and become the next Queen of Persia. Her efforts paid off as she was promoted to his inner court where she was used by God to deliver her people from mass genocide.

One of the hardest working people in the New Testament was the Apostle Paul. He was a brilliant, well-trained rabbi who was thoroughly ambitious. Once God reined in his energies and propelled them in the proper direction, Paul's skills were put to great use. Though he considered all his attainments to be garbage in comparison to knowing Christ (Philippians 3:4–8), God used him to spread the Gospel to the Gentiles and to write at least thirteen books of the New Testament. His extensive theological background enabled him to write things very few could have penned. Paul took no pride in his efforts, but they were of great value to the Kingdom.

That perspective sums up God's thoughts on this topic. Human effort and training are useful in God's service, but the exerciser of the gifts must exhibit holy character. God cares about the heart, but also about the mind and body. It's not acceptable to merely board the train to glory, checking out of world affairs and human competition. Job, Abraham, and Samuel did not get to where they were by sitting on their duffs. Yes, God uses the unlearned through supernatural intervention (fishermen apostles), but Matthew was an established money manager, Luke was a qualified physician, and Lydia was an experienced merchant and accomplished businesswoman.

The Apostle Paul was upset with the believers in the Corinthian church for a number of reasons, one of which was their inability to settle legal disputes between themselves. He expected them to be more intelligent human beings, and reprimanded them, saying:

> *Don't you realize that someday we believers will judge the world? And since you are going to judge the world, can't you decide even these little things among yourselves? Don't you realize that we will judge angels? So you should surely be able to resolve ordinary disputes in this life...Isn't there anyone in all the church who is wise enough to decide these issues?* (1 Corinthians 6:2–5)

Not only should believers strive to balance heart matters with excellence in personal achievement and acumen, but our bodies demand proper attention. The New Testament teaches us that *"the Lord cares about our bodies"* because they were made for him (1 Corinthians 6:13). *"Don't you realize that your body is the temple of the Holy Spirit...for God bought you with a high price. So you must honor God with your body"* (1 Corinthians 6:19–20). What would it mean for us to honor God with our bodies?

Listen again to Paul:

> *Don't you realize that in a race everyone runs, but only one person gets the prize? So run to win! All athletes are disciplined in their training. They do it to win a prize that will fade away, but we do it for an eternal prize. So I run with purpose in every step. I am not just shadowboxing. I discipline my body like an athlete, training it to do what it should. Otherwise, I fear that after preaching to others I myself might be disqualified* (1 Corinthians 9:24–27).

Running to win, running with a purpose, disciplining my body—the duty of man is tough work. Much is required in all fields—heart, mind, and body. When God created us, he was thinking big, not small. His dreams for us are generous. Yes, we are microscopic in comparison to the Almighty, but he wants us to achieve big things within his purposes.

What are mere mortals that you should think about them, human beings that you should care for them? Yet you made them only a little lower than God and crowned them with glory and honor. You gave them charge of everything you made, putting all things under their authority (Psalm 8:4–6).

This passage does not permit us to lazily shuffle around in our bedroom slippers, waiting for our bus to depart for Heaven. We need to get moving, doing, and building here on Earth. We need to study and train. We need to take care of our bodies. We need to shoot for higher targets. We've been put in charge of everything God has made.

Certainly, *"Unless the Lord builds a house, the work of the builders is wasted"* (Psalm 127:1). We need to avoid those earthly exploits that are only about ourselves. But we must vigorously pursue those great earthly exploits which are aligned with God's purposes as we love and worship him with fully devoted hearts.

This is the balance for which we must strive.

DISCUSSION QUESTIONS

1. What does it mean to think one-dimensionally regarding man's purpose on Earth?

2. List some great earthly achievements of the earliest men in Genesis.

3. What is the key difference between the constructions of Noah's Ark and the Tower of Babel?

4. How did Moses exemplify the consummate well-rounded person?

5. What do the constructions of the Tabernacle and the Temple teach us about God's attitude towards excellence in human achievement?

6. How important is polished well-performed musical worship in church?

7. What do other biblical characters teach us about excellence in mind, body, and heart?

8. What does it mean for a believer to live a rich and multi-dimensional life to God's glory?

Chapter 14

"I do some of my best work on mountains."

"He makes me as surefooted as a deer,
enabling me to stand on mountain heights."

~ 2 Samuel 22:34

Mountains are spectacular, breath-taking at times. We love to gaze at them, photograph them, and visit them on holidays. Some of my best family vacations, both as a child and as an adult, involved trips to the mountains. Two of my favorite mountain vistas are found in Yosemite and Glacier National Parks. I particularly love the view heading south on the *Going to the Sun Road* in Montana.

Not only are mountains impressive and magnificent, but they're also great getaways. We often view mountains as a retreat from the real world, from what supposedly really matters. We perceive our everyday lives as true reality. Trips to the mountains are an escape from that—a temporary flight from the important things in life such as business deals, stock purchases, and house renovations. A mountain vacation can seem light and trivial compared to the rigors of the real world of daily life.

In God's paradigm, however, mountains seem to play a different role. They are not the place to *escape* from what supposedly really matters, but rather the place to go to *experience* true reality. For God, real life happens on mountains. In fact, reading his Word could lead one to conclude that he does some of his best spiritual work on mountains.

In God's mind, mountains are settings of challenge, true learning, and growth. They are places to rise above the crowd, the blur, and the whirling corporate world. They are places where our heads can stop spinning for a while, and where we can see things more clearly, maybe even breathe easier. The panoramic view and the fresh mountain air metaphorically represent increased spiritual vision and the invigorating work of the Almighty in our lives when we separate ourselves from the hustle and bustle of the grind.

Jesus liked to do that. The Scriptures record him as often slipping out to a lonely place to pray (Mark 1:35; Luke 5:16). On several occasions, Jesus went to the mountains to fellowship with his Heavenly Father (Mark 6:46; Luke 6:12). One time, he took his closest friends up a mountain and gave them an experience they would never forget:

> *Jesus took Peter and the two brothers, James and John, and led them up a high mountain to be alone. As the men watched, Jesus' appearance was transformed so that his face shone like the sun, and his clothes became as white as light. Suddenly, Moses and Elijah appeared and began talking with Jesus* (Matthew 17:1–3).

Besides this incident on the Mount of Transfiguration (Mount Tabor?), the Bible describes many significant spiritual events occurring on mountains. At the end of the Flood, Noah's ark came to rest on the Mountains of Ararat (Genesis 8:4). There he offered sacrifices to God and received the Lord's promise to never again destroy the Earth with water (Genesis 9:15).

When the Lord promised Abraham that he would be a great nation and his descendants would possess the entire land of Canaan, he did so on Mount Hazor, a high plateau situated in between Bethel and Ai (Genesis 12:8 cf. 13:14–17). From this vantage point, Abraham could easily view the whole length and width of the land. And when Abraham was given his supreme test of faith regarding the sacrifice of his son Isaac, he was commanded by God to do so on top of Mount Moriah (Genesis 22:2).

Mountains played a key role in the history of the Israelites as well. It was on Mount Horeb that Moses first met God in the burning bush (Exodus 3:1–2). Years later, on this same mountain, also referred to as Mount Sinai, God delivered the Ten Commandments and the rest of the Law to his chosen people. There he also established a covenant with them, promising to bless them as long as they remained faithfully obedient to him (Deuteronomy 4:9–40). Horeb was also the place where Moses struck the rock that brought forth water to satisfy the thirst of the disgruntled Jewish congregation (Exodus 17:6).

High atop Mounts Pisgah and Peor, the prophet Balaam received words of blessing from God for the children of Israel even though he had been hired specifically by King Balak to curse them (Number 23:13–24:9).

Before the Israelites entered the Promised Land, brothers Aaron and Moses finished their earthly lives on top of mountains and went to be with the Lord. *"While they were at the foot of Mount Hor, Aaron the priest was directed by the Lord to go up the mountain, and there he died"* (Numbers 33:38). Later in the same year, the younger sibling met his Maker also.

> *Then Moses went up to Mount Nebo from the plains of Moab and climbed Pisgah Peak, which is across from Jericho. And the Lord showed him the whole land...Then the Lord said to Moses, "This is the land I promised on oath to Abraham...I have now allowed you to see it with your own eyes, but you will not enter the land." So Moses, the servant of the Lord, died there in the land of Moab, just as the Lord had said* (Deuteronomy 34:1–5).

Under Israel's next generation of leadership, mountains continued to serve as significant places for God's work amidst his people. At the twin mountains between the Mediterranean Sea and the River Jordan in Samaria, Mount Gerizim and Mount Ebal, Joshua assembled the tribes of Israel to instruct them in the Law of Moses (Joshua 8:30–35). It was from these mountains that God's blessings (from Mount Gerizim) and curses (from Mount Ebal) fell upon the chosen people (Deuteronomy 11:29).

Up until the time of Christ, Mount Gerizim was considered sacred to the Samaritans, who, as stated by the woman at the well, regularly *"worshipped in this mountain"* (John 4:20 NASB). To the Jews, Mount Zion was their primary interest. King David had seized Zion from the Jebusites (Joshua 15:63; 2 Samuel 5:7) and eventually built his palace on top of it, thereby designating Jerusalem as the 'City of David'.

One cannot read the Old Testament without being intrigued by the story of the prophet Elijah on Mount Carmel (1 Kings 18). There he courageously confronted hundreds of hostile false prophets of Baal, miraculously demonstrating the veracity of the one true God whose name is Jehovah. Those who witnessed that mountaintop episode must have been forever changed—watching fire from Heaven consume not only the meat, but the stones of the altar itself, as well as buckets of water. Their response that day was, *"The Lord—he is God! Yes, the Lord is God"* (1 Kings 18:39).

This prominent role of mountains in the work of God carried into the New Testament. Part of Jesus' temptation involved the devil bringing the Lord to a very high mountain to show him all the kingdoms of the Earth for the taking if he was willing to bow down to Satan (Matthew 4:8). Christ was, of course, victorious over the temptation and came down from the mountain ready to commence his public ministry in the strength of his Heavenly Father.

When he first called his disciples to follow him, Jesus summoned them to come away for a while and go up a mountain with him (Mark 3:13). He preached from mountains (Matthew 5:1), created feasts out of table scraps for thousands on a mountain (Matthew15:29–38), was crucified on a mountain, and delivered the Great Commission from atop a mountain (Matthew 28:16–20).

Specific mountains played key roles in Jesus' ministry. Northern Palestine's Mount Hermon appears to be the setting where he revealed to his disciples his plan to build his church, as well as his intention to go back to Jerusalem where he would die and be resurrected (Matthew 16:13–21).

The Mount of Olives was the place where Jesus stood when he wept over Jerusalem and then later delivered the Olivet discourse, prophesying about Israel's future and the end times (Matthew 24–25). In the final days before his crucifixion, Luke referred to Jesus teaching daily in the Temple and then retiring to the Mount of Olives at night (Luke 21:37). The seclusion from the hubbub of the city must have been a welcome invitation for the Galilean after a full day of teaching.

After the Last Supper, Jesus went with his disciples to the Mount of Olives (Matthew 26:30) where he was eventually betrayed (Matthew 26:47–56). After his resurrection, Jesus ascended to Heaven from the Mount of Olives, promising to return to the same location in the future (Acts 1:9–12). This event will, one day, fulfill Zechariah's prophecy stating that a final battle between the Messiah and his opponents will take place on this very same mountain (Zechariah 14:1–4).

Having seen the significant role mountains have played in the revelation of God to man over the years, it's no surprise that the Apostle John, as recorded in the Book of Revelation, was taken away to a great and high mountain to prophetically witness the New Jerusalem coming down to Earth out of Heaven in the end times (21:10).

So besides a little geographical education, what is the point of this discussion? As the Scriptures reveal, mountains seem to play a crucial role in God's relationship with mankind. Key developments in the realization of his Kingdom transpire in areas of higher elevation. Why is that?

In and of themselves, mountains seem to have a healthier flavour—more natural, less civilized. Cultural progress advances in valleys, but spiritual growth more readily comes on mountaintops. Besides, there seems to be more darkness in valleys (Psalm 23:4), and certainly more sin—the Valley of Siddim where Sodom and Gomorrah were located, the San Fernando Valley (i.e. Porn Valley).

As humans, we need all the help we can get to connect meaningfully with God. We are so easily deceived and distracted. The routines of life, most with little eternal value, consume our thoughts, passions, and bank accounts. We need some place different, some place higher, to rise above the scamper and commotion of life in order to meet with God. We need a new perspective that comes with being apart from the habitual schedule. A mountain seems to be able to provide that. A higher position brings clearer vision, a broader outlook, and more lucid thinking.

Biblical characters Daniel and Peter are both noted as going to the highest part of their houses when they wanted to meet God in prayer (Daniel 6:10; Acts 10:9). When I lived in Ontario, we owned a two-and-a-half storey Victorian home that had a captivating view from the attic window. I loved to sit there, looking out over the neighborhood from that high vantage point, talking with God.

Where is the mountain in your life that takes you away from the scuttle? For many, like me living on the prairies, physical mountains are a rare commodity. I experience some form of transcendent inspiration when I sporadically make my way to the panoramic peaks of Alberta and British Columbia, but that is not where I live the majority of my life. Ninety-nine percent of the time, I am staring at big flat horizons.

For most, mountaintop experiences must be metaphorical. But that does not preclude their importance. Routinely, we need to find some place to rise above the rush and meet with God. For prairie folk like me, that could be an encounter with a gorgeous sunset or a prolonged gaze into the rapturous cloud patterns of our big skies. Perhaps your mountain experience is a special place you like to go by yourself—a closet, a cove, a creek, a comfortable reading chair. Maybe it's your daily commute where you talk with the Lord or listen to Scripture on your iPod. Possibly it's your gym workout or your walk with the dog. For some, institutional church services elevate the worshiper to fellowship with the Almighty, prompting transformation of character. Others escape the ordinary through times of scheduled prayer, small group study, or personal journaling. Some even find their mountain experiences through athletics, where a weekly pick-up hockey or basketball game generates more worship than sweat.

Where you find your mountain meeting with God is immaterial. The fact that you need one is essential. Jesus told his followers, *"But when you pray, go away by yourself, shut the door behind you, and pray to your Father in private"* (Matthew 6:6).We need to hear the voice of God like Moses did on Mount Sinai, away from the noisy crowd and the din of the television set. When we feel disheartened or depressed, we need the encouragement God provides like he gave to Elijah on Mount Horeb (1 Kings 19:8–18).

A human perspective sees mountains as a temporary reprieve from the daily grind, a place for casual recreation apart from the real world. God sees mountains, both physical and metaphorical, as necessary places to gain spiritual rest and enrichment, so that we may grow deeper in matters that really count. Today, God may be telling us that we can learn a lot on a mountain; in fact, it seems like that's where he does some of his best spiritual work in our lives.

DISCUSSION QUESTIONS

1. From a human perspective, how are mountains typically viewed?

2. What role did mountains play in Jesus' ministry?

3. In your opinion, what is the most intriguing mountaintop experience in the Bible?

4. Why is Mount Sinai significant in the Old Testament narrative?

5. Why is the Mount of Olives significant in the Bible?

6. Is life truly healthier up on the mountains and more sinful down in the valleys?

7. Where in their lives might people find metaphorical mountains of spiritual retreat?

8. Do we really need a 'mountain' in our lives to gain spiritual rest and enrichment?

Chapter 15

"Yah, you're right.
I am a little old-fashioned."

"Ask for the old, godly way, and walk in it."

~ Jeremiah 6:16

Pop quiz—why are we so infatuated with things that are new? From a human perspective, new always seems better than old. Sometimes it's true. My new Accord is safer and gets better mileage than the old sedans of the 1950's. Today's hand-held devices are certainly an improvement over the elephantine computers we had when I was in high school. Taupe is definitely more attractive than turquoise. And when pocket-sized electronic calculators hit the market in the 1970's, they performed only four basic functions and cost $100. Yes, new can be better…but not always.

Often the quest for something new can lead to complications and heart-ache—like the search for a new lover when we're already married, or the pursuit of a promising new career that turns out to be a huge mistake. Entrenched in the fallen human paradigm is an illusion—if only I could get that new _____, then I'd be happy. As I watch late night TV infomercials, I muse, "That new exercise bike could help me finally lose those twenty extra pounds insulating my mid-section." It's easy to trust in a new person, possession, or event to alleviate the suffering from past mistakes or shortcomings.

But time and again, we experience the piercing disappointment of success. We envision something new, passionately pursue it, only to discover that the elation is short-lived. Or worse, we realize the old we used to have is actually better than what we have now. Think Vista vs. XP. I wonder how many people have bought new homes they didn't need just because they chased that burning desire to experience something different.

As Jeremiah 2:13 explains, we are wired for intimacy with God and for what he provides, but we naturally search for satisfaction in places other than God to quench our thirst. Jeremiah likened this to digging a bunch of useless broken wells. One of the cisterns that we commonly dig is the ongoing quest for something new and fresh. We are attracted to the new because it feels exciting and has the sense of possibility and opportunity.

Nowhere do we see this more abundantly than in the world of fashion. Designers and photographers fall over each other to create and publicize the hottest new fashions. Possessing the most recent designer label jeans somehow makes us more attractive, superior to those who still wear Wranglers. Being up on the latest fashion craze seems to position us better for promotion, or at least elevates our overall chic factor.

Women's hemlines and necklines rise and fall like insurance company stock. Men's ties contract and expand like celebrities on and off their diets. Is there truly anything new in fashion? Has it not all been done before? Do we really need 354 different brands of shoes?[22] Is life somehow better with new Etnies instead of old Reeboks?

Another domain intoxicated with 'newer is better' is the field of education. I've seen a few merry-go-rounds in my

---

[22] Cited June 12, 2010 http://www.shoesreview.net/sitemap.php

educational career—school calendar experiments, semestering vs. all year classes, open classrooms vs. traditional buildings. Teachers are introduced to a lot of 'new' ideas that are not actually new. We go in cycles. We forget about something for a while until it re-emerges as a novel approach or a ground-breaking new concept. For instance, the open classroom model, popular in the United States in the 1970's, was actually a derivation of the old one-room schoolhouse.

For three decades, I have witnessed the emergence of countless educational reforms, always with the message that help has finally arrived. Even when nothing is broken, a fix is prescribed. Every new idea in education is touted as being *the one* that will really work this time, as opposed to all the old deplorable practices that have failed so miserably in the past.

Today, educational reform is running on all cylinders—outcomes based education (OBE), No Child Left Behind (NCLB), data driven learning, constructivist learning theory, and the whole re-creation of assessment. I'm not opposed to much of the content and philosophy of many new reforms, but I am offended by the way they are presented—as something truly novel, and guaranteed to produce the results we have waited for so long.

Listening to my colleagues south of the border, it appears NCLB is not working very well. And from a standpoint of the novelty factor, much of the new plan is just old ideas repackaged. Outcomes based education is not that new; it's been around since the 1980's. The concepts of self-directed learning, indirect teaching, and precisely meeting the needs of a child are Montessori notions that have existed for one hundred years. The model of children learning by doing was purported by John Dewey in the late nineteenth century. Citizenship training and experience-based education were promoted by Rousseau in the eighteenth century. The Socratic method of teaching is named after a Greek guy who lived over 2400 years ago.

Bottom line, there is no single reform that will establish Camelot in our nations' schools. Regardless of educational philosophy or the period of history, good teachers have always been teaching well—knowing their material, understanding the needs of their students, tailoring the learning as best they can to those individual needs, making children feel safe and secure in the learning environment, making learning relevant, and loving life through learning.

Educational reform has been discussed at some length here because it is a perfect illustration of this human infatuation with the concept of newer always being better. That is not how God thinks. We'll get to that later.

I will say it again. Of course, newer can sometimes be better. Our attitudes towards the environment and personal health are markedly superior to that of our predecessors. But on the other hand, sometimes the old ways are superior and should be retained. Perhaps you have experienced this in your own work situation. When facing the challenges of the new economy, corporations without a solid sustenance plan repeatedly put their charges through painful fiascos of re-alignment and new structuring that amount to nothing more than re-arranging the deck chairs on the Titanic. Nothing meaningfully new is being accomplished.

I have found that people who resist change are often deemed lazy, unprogressive, and stubborn. Occasionally this is true. But there may be another option. Perhaps these 'heel-draggers' are convinced that some of the older ideas and methods are actually better. Perhaps they see these emerging new ideas as lacking substance, or as nothing new at all.

Much of our human tendency to hunt for the new is rooted in the theory of evolution. An evolutionary paradigm views the human race as continually progressing, driving us to secure the next new thing that will make us better and stronger, more fit for survival. Evolutionary theory subtly implies that we need something fresh to keep moving up in order to reach our full human potential.

Such man-focused thinking has never worked, ever. By ourselves, we cannot improve. Truthfully, we can't do anything apart from Christ, in that he holds the molecules of our brains and bodies together by the word of his power (Colossians 1:17). New ideas that are humanistic in nature will take us somewhere, but not necessarily where we need to go. We need to become more holy. Left to our own devices, we usually get worse. Such was the case for the Jewish nation throughout much of its history.

Twenty-six hundred years ago, Nebuchadnezzar was bearing down on the children of Israel as part of a divinely ordained punishment for the errant nation. The Babylonian king was threatening to invade Palestine in order to capture its best and brightest, destroy their capital city, and wipe out anyone who opposed them. God was using a foreign, unbelieving world leader to bring judgment upon his own chosen people, the Israelites, because they had been terribly disobedient and unfaithful to the Lord. God had given them many warnings through his prophets to smarten up and start obeying, but they refused.

The Book of Jeremiah tells the story of Israel's last days in the Promised Land before they were invaded and their capital city flattened. If you want to get a glimpse of the condition of their rebellious hearts before this judgment, listen to the Word of God as recorded by his prophet:

For my people have done two evil things: They have abandoned me—the fountain of living water. And they have dug for themselves cracked cisterns that can hold no water at all! (2:13)

No amount of soap or lye can make you clean. I still see the stain of your guilt. I, the Sovereign Lord, have spoken! (2:22)

"My people are foolish and do not know me," says the Lord. "They are stupid children who have no

understanding. They are clever enough at doing wrong, but they have no idea how to do right!" (4:22)

A horrible and shocking thing has happened in this land—the prophets give false prophecies, and the priests rule with an iron hand. Worse yet, my people like it that way (5:30–31).

Are they ashamed of their disgusting actions? Not at all— they don't even know how to blush! (6:15)

These are very harsh words. Instead of being a light to the world, a shining beacon of hope to other nations because of the presence of the one true God in their midst, the Israelites were a mess. They mocked God's presence and ignored his salvation by forsaking his Word and following the selfish desires of their own hearts.

Yet in the midst of their rebellion and spiritual apathy, on the eve of their impending destruction, the Book of Jeremiah records numerous pleas from God for their repentance. One such call for them to get their act together is found in Jeremiah 6:16. The exhortation is in the symbolic language befitting a traveler on a long and challenging journey. *"This is what the Lord says: 'Stop at the crossroads and look around. Ask for the old, godly way, and walk in it. Travel its path, and you will find rest for your souls.'"*

The implication is that, on our own, we are a tad lost. The Lord tells us to stop right where we are, and look for the old, godly way. Another version says it this way: *"See and ask for the ancient paths, where the good way is"* (NASB). There are many paths to choose from in life and we need to pick the right road, no matter how old it is.

As I travel with my wife, I behave like a typical male who resists asking for help when looking for a particular destination. I believe that if I just drive around long enough, I will eventually find what I'm looking for. When I do this, my wife becomes convinced that I am an idiot because she just wants me to stop and ask the people on the sidewalk for help.

One time in Calgary, we were searching for our friend's house. They live in one of those new subdivisions where every street has some variation of the same name. Naturally, we didn't have any success until I finally stopped and asked for help. And then, of course, we immediately found the right way, the true way, the only way that mattered.

God challenges us, in the midst of many paths, to look for the old, godly way. Seek it out!

But living in today's post-modern culture, those words— *"the old, godly way"*—do not sound very attractive. As we have already discussed, there is not a great deal of respect for old things today. It's really too bad. Why do we have this delusion that 'old' means useless?

Even our perception of 'old' has radically changed. When I was a kid, I played with the same toys for years. Technological gadgets are now considered old within months, not years or decades. And this plethora of gadgetry, though amusing to fiddle with, still fails to improve us deeply. We're more connected, but less intimate. We're more informed, but continue to act dumber. We have everything at our fingertips, but we've never been so jaded.

We may do things differently and interact with people and machines in new ways, but in the end, humans do only two things in life: we either love God or we love the world. We either follow the Lord or we practice sin. There are only two options. That's the way it is and that's the way it's always been. Three thousand years ago, the author of Ecclesiastes said:

> *Everything is wearisome beyond description. No matter how much we see, we are never satisfied. No matter how much we hear, we are not content. History merely repeats itself. It has all been done before. Nothing under the sun is truly new. Sometimes people say, "Here is something new!" But actually it is old; nothing is ever truly new* (Ecclesiastes 1:8–10).

You may be offered new and supposedly exciting paths to explore, but the only one that will bring lasting joy and *"rest for your soul"* (Jeremiah 6:16) is the old, godly way. At the end of his life-learning treatise, the Teacher in Ecclesiastes summed up the old, godly way in the following straightforward manner: *"Fear God and obey his commandments"* (Ecclesiastes 12:13). That is the crux of the matter.

But choosing to walk the old, godly way does not necessitate a life that is out of date or boring. The old, godly way is the path of trusting God for everything and walking obediently according to his Word and in his power. It's an exciting road. For centuries, this road of faith has been navigated by many great men and women who have done amazing things in God's Kingdom. It was walked by Abel, Enoch, Noah, Abraham, Joseph, Moses, Joshua, Rahab, Gideon, Samson, David, and the Old Testament prophets. The old, godly way is the path that was chosen by Jesus' disciples, the Apostle Paul, Luke, and Barnabas.

You can walk in the old, godly way and still be contemporary. The Gospel does not instruct us to be out of touch and socially inept. A godly life grows out of an intimate relationship with Jesus Christ, as he carries us through the many challenges and rewards of life. Those who have travelled this path will testify that the old, godly way is also the most refreshing, invigorating, and interesting one we can take.

It's also the safest. We may not acknowledge the fact, but apart from the old, godly way, we are headed for destruction. Even some people who go to church regularly are in trouble. If we are relying on our Christian heritage and church attendance to make us right before God, we are not on the right path. If we think our cutting-edge emerging theology is guaranteeing our standing in Heaven, we are sorely mistaken. The Gospel message has not changed. The old, godly way involves a walk with Jesus that costs us everything.

Just because we know the other members, the songs, the routines, the dress code, and the seating plan in the pews doesn't assure us we are actually doing it right. Just because we are comfortable in church doesn't guarantee that we are progressing down the old, godly way. Being a true disciple of Jesus means a lot more than just uttering a little sinner's prayer around a campfire at the age of twelve; it's about total immersion in the work of God's Kingdom, aiming at very high standards, entire submission to the Master, and bearing genuine fruit.

Some religious people in Jeremiah's day had the same faulty impression that walking with God simply involved a weak commitment to the program, something like signing up for a membership and then doing whatever you please. Jeremiah rebuked them for their poor judgment:

> *Don't be fooled into thinking that you will never suffer because the Temple is here. It's a lie! Do you really think you can steal, murder, commit adultery, lie, and burn incense to Baal and all those other new gods of yours, and then come here and stand before me in my Temple and chant, "We are safe!"—only to go right back to all those evils again?* (Jeremiah 7:8–10)

Just chanting, "We're safe because we're in the Temple" is no guarantee of safety. A Christian is one who trusts God for their salvation and obeys his Word. A true Christian travels the path of godliness and does not just talk about it. A true Christian is one who is radically committed to Jesus Christ. If we do not walk the old, godly way, we are not nearly as safe as we think we are, inside or outside of church.

Eternal destinies are at stake here, but so is the quality of life now. When we walk this path with God, we will find rest for our souls. How tragic that our response would be the same as the Israelites 2600 years ago. Notice the very last phrase of Jeremiah 6:16. *"Stop at the crossroads and look around. Ask for the old, godly way, and walk in it. Travel its path, and you will find rest for your souls. But you reply, 'No, that's not the road we want!'"* (Jeremiah 6:16)

God offers rest for the soul and yet many say they're not interested. They'd rather be independent of God. They'd rather run their own show and be enamored with new-fangled things, check out new paths, and explore fresh options. We are all free to make that choice, but we need to understand the outcome of such a decision.

To think like God is to be a bit more deliberate with everything new that comes our way. We cannot be so naïve as to think that all advancements bring improvement. The prospect of something new has the aura of excitement, but we need to take a sober second look and make sure that what is being pursued is not something that strays us off the old, godly way.

When we encounter a novel prospect or innovative idea, we need to ask the right questions. How does it help us be better people? How does it fit in with the fact that eventually the Kingdom of God is going to rule every nook and cranny of the Universe? Will a commitment to this philosophy, technology, or lifestyle change bring rest or stress to our souls? Will it help or hinder our focus on the priority of the old Gospel message? Does it take into account the power of God that is intended and available to strengthen and purify our lives?

DISCUSSION QUESTIONS

1. Why are we so infatuated with things that are new?
2. How may we actually diminish our lives by repeatedly pursuing the 'next new thing'?
3. What do you think is the best illustration of 'newer is not necessarily better'?
4. What was Jeremiah's antidote for the sinfulness of his Jewish contemporaries in 6th century B.C.?
5. What are the benefits of walking in the old godly way?
6. What does the Book of Ecclesiastes have to say about the allure of new things in life?
7. "You can walk in the old godly way and still be contemporary." Agree or disagree.
8. How should a Christian properly determine the value of a new idea or opportunity in life?

Chapter 16

"I hope you don't mind that I can be a little mysterious."

"The Lord our God has secrets known to no one. We are not accountable for them, but we and our children are accountable forever for all that he has revealed to us."

~ Deuteronomy 29:29

No matter how long we have been on the road of pursuing God, we may still be tempted to put him in a box. It's only natural—we want to understand him and what he's doing. We want to explain him to others who are also wondering about the methods and mechanism of the Almighty. After all, that is the whole point of this book—tearing out the human predispositions of our minds and replacing them with a divine paradigm.

But part of understanding how God thinks involves occasional concessions on our part. There are times when we need to release him to be who he is without us 'getting it'. There are times when we simply need to accept the puzzling facts before us and give up our obsession with figuring things out. German sociologist Georg Simmel wrote, "Every superior personality, and every superior performance, has, for the average of mankind, something mysterious."[23] How much more so for the Lord of the Universe?

The mysteries of God's ways are inherent throughout all Scripture, but sometimes it's useful to focus in on a single biblical narrative to discover some specific secrets God may want us to acknowledge yet not comprehend. Sometimes we see things clearly. Other times, we are beckoned to peer into the shadows and embrace the obscure parts of our Heavenly Father by faith.

As we now venture into enigmatic territory, understand that the value in this exercise is not that we'll solve the ambiguity, but simply that we'll understand more clearly what the mysteries are. Sometimes, putting the riddle into clearer words is all we need to do.

One of the earliest narratives in the New Testament is laden with mysteries of divine operation. Consider the story of the magi coming to visit the newborn Christ. The Christian church referred to this event as Epiphany. January 6, the twelfth day after Christmas, is the official day of Epiphany. Historically, this day included feasting and a commemoration of the revelation of Jesus to humanity.

You see, it is through the magi that Christ is manifested to the world as the Savior of all mankind, both Jew and Gentile. The wise men, as we tend to call them, revealed Jesus to the world as both Lord and King, and as Simeon said in Luke 2:32, *"a light to reveal God to the nations."*

The word epiphany means to show forth, to make known, or to reveal. Apart from the Christmas season, it's common to use the word epiphany to describe that moment when there is an intuitive realization of the meaning of something, when the lights go on inside someone's head, arousing the response—"I get it!" "I've had an epiphany!"

Let us consider this very familiar story of the magi in the hope that we will see something new and fresh in it, that we

---

[23] Cited April 10, 2010 http://www.brainyquote.com/quotes/
keywords/mysterious.html

may even experience our own little epiphany, our own little personal revelation of how God mysteriously works in humanity.

A close examination of this story recorded in Matthew 2 reveals that there are at least three divine mysteries nestled within the account. Familiarity with the story precludes the need to quote the text here.

The first mystery in the story of the magi is a kind of double mystery—why does God choose *these* men to make this journey, and why is *Matthew* the one telling us this story at all?

We don't know much about these visitors from the East. We call them kings, but Matthew called them magi, best understood as belonging to a caste of wise men specializing in astrology, medicine, and natural science. We think of them as astrologers because they were observing stars, and astrology was considered a learned occupation in that eastern culture.

Interestingly enough, the Greek word translated 'magi' here in Matthew also shows up twice in the Book of Acts (8:9–24; 13:6–11) where it is translated magician or sorcerer. Contemporary Jewish perspective would have considered magi to be pagans who looked to the stars for answers that legitimately should come from God, or unbelievers who worked magic using demonic powers.

The characters in our story were inherently far from the Kingdom, which mysteriously made them useful to God as he showed that, through Jesus, he was bringing salvation to those culturally considered beyond the scope of God's interest. These were not the expected beneficiaries of the arrival of the King of the Jews. Yet we see that the birth of Jesus brought about change, a change that involved an inclusivity which troubled those who expected only a traditional Jewish king.

The Good News, or the Gospel, had come in Jesus, but it was not just good news for those who were the good people of God. Jesus was good news for all people, including bad people.

And the other twist of the first mystery is this—why does God have the most Jewish of the Gospel writers include this story of the first Gentiles coming to worship Jesus as the King of all peoples? We know that Matthew's goal is to show Jesus as King of the Jews, as the fulfillment of Jewish Old Testament messianic prophecies. And yet God chose to inspire Matthew to include this very Gentile narrative within his account of the life of Christ. Why wouldn't we hear this story from Luke, the Gentile writer who had a universal perspective on the Gospel message? Time and again, God does not operate like we think he should.

Within this mystery we learn a very distinct part of the mind of God—he chooses unlikely people to do his work. Remember Moses? Remember Gideon? Remember the anointing of King David? How about Nebuchadnezzar, Jonah, or even Hosea's wife? He chooses the people we would probably not choose. We would not likely pick unknown star gazers from a faraway pagan culture to reveal to the world that the King of all mankind had arrived. God selects improbable characters to execute his divine plans.

Quick personal application—have you ever sensed the call of God on your life to do something that you feel you are unqualified for? Do not automatically cringe from the opportunity. Listen to what author Madeline L'Engle writes:

> In a very real sense, not one of us is qualified but it seems that God continually chooses the most unqualified to do His work, to bear His glory. If we are qualified, we tend to think that we have done the job ourselves. If we are forced to accept our evident lack of qualification, then there is no danger that we will confuse God's work with our own – or God's glory with our own.[24]

God chooses unlikely people to do his work. That's the first mystery.

---

[24] Cited April 10, 2010 http://www.goodreads.com/quotes/show/43373

The second mystery is found in the logistics of the magi's excursion and the Bethlehem visit.

At a glance, humanly speaking, one might be tempted to exclaim, "What a waste!" These guys—probably successful in their careers, perhaps family men—left their homes, friends, and country to embark on a long and perplexing journey. This was an expedition that took at least months, perhaps over a year, and had no certain happy ending from their vantage point.

When they arrived in Jerusalem, they were still somewhat confused and looking for help. After talking with King Herod and finding out that Jesus was to be born in Bethlehem, they were thrilled to once again see the same star they'd seen back in the East. And that star took them to the little Messiah. Finally, their journey had come to an end; they arrived at the house where the infant Jesus was living with his parents and they fell down and worshiped him and gave him their treasures. Wow! What an exhausting tale. After months of harsh traveling, they reached their destination. Mission accomplished.

But wait, do they stay there for a while? Do they establish a little Christian community around the Christ Child? Do they hang out and party with Mary and Joseph for a few weeks? It doesn't appear so. In fact, from a simple reading of the text, the dream warning them to go home another way to avoid King Herod sounds like it might have occurred that very night.

I don't want to read more into the text than is there, but Matthew provides no indication that these travelers stayed in Bethlehem very long at all. What if they left to go home the very next day? What if they immediately began their huge journey back east? My human brain says, "What a waste of time and resources!" Was there not a more economical and efficient way this could have been accomplished? Was there not a better use of resources? What if they made the enormous trip to Bethlehem and back, all to spend only a few hours with

Jesus? All of this time and effort and money for only one evening in his presence? I don't get it!

Again, we see the mysterious nature of God and of those who are wholly devoted to him. In God's economy, an attitude of adoration of the Savior can often involve behavior that looks like a waste from a human perspective. But God sees things differently.

About a week before his death, Jesus was invited to the home of Lazarus for dinner. During the meal, Mary poured very expensive perfume over Jesus' feet and the whole house was filled with a beautiful fragrance. A bystander complained about the waste; the perfume used for such an ignoble purpose was worth a year's wages. Wasn't there a better use for such a valuable possession? But even though the costly fragrance was largely dumped out on the ground, Jesus said Mary's behavior was appropriate (John 12:1–8). In God's eyes, this lavish use of resources was a good decision.

The worship of God can often involve a perceived waste of resources.

Think of the lives of many missionaries. How many followers of Christ have been maligned, even by friends and family, for their choice to spend their lives in faraway, even hostile, cultures in an effort to spread the saving message of Jesus to those unreached by the Gospel? How many missionaries have been told they are throwing away their lives when they could be enjoying the comforts of a North American successful career which would, of course, enable them to support others who might be so inclined to go abroad?

My mind goes immediately to the life of John Speers, a good friend of mine from my college days in the late 1970's. He was a great guy—funny, talented, smart. He chose to deposit his life for Christ on the mission field, in a very dangerous environment on a southern island of the Philippines. For that choice, he was murdered by an enraged national who had a hatred for Christians—shot in the back of the head while eating a meal in a restaurant. Some people looking at John Speers' demise might proclaim, "What a waste of a life!" However, God looks at John's short life of thirty-three years and says with pleasure, "Well done, thou good and faithful servant."

This fact begs two questions. How have I ever lavishly poured out my time and resources like the magi in my adoration of the Savior? Does my life and use of assets, devoted to God, cause others to say, "What a waste!"? Mysteriously, that may not necessarily be a bad commentary. The worship of God can often involve the perceived waste of resources. That is the second mystery.

The third mystery in the story is how God puts himself at risk. The narrative tells of a small child whose life is in danger. This vulnerability in the life of the Messiah is not unique to this passage, but it's certainly clear here.

Unlike a typical earthly king, God left himself at our mercy where we could do him harm, even kill him. The angry and hateful actions of a jealous human king sent the Messiah King running, hiding in Egypt until the murderer himself eventually died. Even then, Joseph was forced to take his precious son and wife far away from Judea because Herod's successor also posed a threat to the safety of Jesus.

Even from the very start, as a baby and then as a small child whisked away into hiding, Jesus' task was not one that would be done from strength, but from vulnerability, exposure, and eventually death. God the Father mysteriously crafted it that way.

This is not how a human would script the revelation of a Savior for the world. We would make him stronger and less susceptible to harm. But God made him weak.

And mysteriously, even today, God puts himself at risk as he entrusts himself to frail beings who flail away in their humanity, seeking to follow the Savior. Jesus is still susceptible to assaults and criticisms as he resides in our hearts and is held responsible for our mistakes and our hypocrisies. Why does God continue to put himself at risk and make himself vulnerable by entrusting his reputation to humans? It is a mystery, but it's the way God does it and so it is right.

If we want to walk appropriately as children of God, we have a better chance of behaving properly in the eyes of God when we begin to understand the mind of God. And part of understanding the mind of God is embracing the mysteries that lie therein. Some of those mysteries are found in the story of the magi:

- God chooses unlikely people to do his work

- The worship of Christ can involve the perceived waste of resources

- God puts himself at risk by subjecting himself to human vessels

Perhaps these thoughts may awaken within your heart a deeper epiphany, or revelation, of the nature of God. Learn to embrace these mysteries and see where God takes you.

DISCUSSION QUESTIONS

1. How should we respond to those aspects of God's ways that are mysterious or confusing?

2. Why is it odd that God chose the magi to play a part in revealing Christ to the world?

3. What is strange about Matthew being the one to record the story of the magi?

4. From a human perspective, how might the magi's journey be considered wasteful?

5. How else is this concept of lavish or wasteful worship illustrated in the New Testament?

6. How might some believers today be viewed by others as 'wasting their lives'?

7. How is God vulnerable in the story of Jesus' birth?

8. How does God continue to put himself at risk today?

Chapter 17

"What do you want to be saved from?"

*"The crowds that went ahead of him and those that
followed shouted, 'Hosanna to the Son of David!
Blessed is he who comes in the name of the Lord!
Hosanna in the highest!'"*

~ Matthew 21:9 NIV

Matthew tells an incredible story of Jesus' Triumphal
Entry into the city of Jerusalem five days before he was
murdered:

*As they approached Jerusalem and came to Bethphage on
the Mount of Olives, Jesus sent two disciples, saying to
them, "Go to the village ahead of you, and at once you will
find a donkey tied there, with her colt by her. Untie them
and bring them to me. If anyone says anything to you, tell
him that the Lord needs them, and he will send them right
away." This took place to fulfill what was spoken through
the prophet: "Say to the Daughter of Zion, 'See, your king
comes to you, gentle and riding on a donkey, on a colt, the
foal of a donkey.'" The disciples went and did as Jesus had
instructed them. They brought the donkey and the colt,
placed their cloaks on them, and Jesus sat on them. A very
large crowd spread their cloaks on the road, while others
cut branches from the trees and spread them on the road.*

*The crowds that went ahead of him and those that followed
shouted, "Hosanna to the Son of David! Blessed is he who
comes in the name of the Lord! Hosanna in the highest!"
When Jesus entered Jerusalem, the whole city was stirred
and asked, "Who is this?" The crowds answered, "This is
Jesus, the prophet from Nazareth in Galilee"* (Matthew
21:1–11 NIV).

A king rides into Jerusalem on a little donkey. What is
going on? What kind of king is this? Like most of Jesus'
stories, something is odd. Something twists, or just isn't what
we expect. Filthy shepherds get the first press release on his
arrival to Earth. The rotten son is welcomed back with a
banquet. Spit is used to return sight. The enemy Samaritan is
the one who helps rather than the priest. Very often, stories
involving Jesus do not readily make sense to human thinking.
When the King of Kings made his Triumphal Entry into
Jerusalem on what we traditionally call Palm Sunday, the
people's expectations were about to get challenged.

For most of his ministry, Jesus' followers had been
anxious for him to take up the trappings of kingship. The
heavenly message accompanying his birth stated that he was
indeed the Savior, the Messiah, the King of the Jews. His life,
character, and miracles testified to the fact that he was the real
deal, God's deliverer to mankind. After years of Roman
occupation, the Jews were hungry for some deliverance.
Imagine their excitement when they saw his disciples
signaling that today was the day. A procession was forming.
The King was arriving. He could have walked, but he didn't.
He was riding. Jesus was entering Jerusalem through the main
gate, laying claim to the city. Their wait was over; their lives
were about to improve. They were going to be delivered. The
Romans were going to get what was coming to them.

And yet they should have known that something did not
jive. Something was not quite right. True, there was a
precedent—when Solomon became king, he rode David's
favorite mule during the inaugural procession into Jerusalem

(1 Kings 1:33). Now, Jesus was riding into Jerusalem like a conquering king. But he was on a baby donkey, so young and little it needed its mother close by (Matthew 21:2). If he were indeed a conquering king, would he not have ridden into the city on a fearsome warhorse, or in a gilded chariot? And yet Jesus specified that his transportation needed to be a young colt that had never been ridden.

According to Jewish law, the only animals used for sacred purposes were those which had never been employed as beasts of burden (Numbers 19:2; 1 Samuel 6:7). This indeed was primarily a sacred occasion, not a political one. It was a sacred event because it was going to involve a sacrifice. But no one was thinking about that on this day. And so, with limited and faulty understanding, the disciples fired up the party.

Up to this point, Jesus had avoided publicity, not wanting people to know he was the Messiah. Nor had he wanted to provoke the Jewish leaders who for some time had been plotting to kill him. *"My hour is not yet come"* (John 2:4 NASB), he told people during his ministry, not wanting to reveal his true identity too early. But now, Jesus knew that the hour of his death was at hand.

Unlike all other occasions up to this point, Jesus was now accepting the title of 'King'. The disciples had deeply longed for this, but really wondered if it would ever happen. Once they realized what was going down, they did all they could to make this a truly royal procession. They draped their cloaks over the donkey's back to make Jesus more comfortable, and to make the donkey more presentable.

The city was alive with anticipation. Soon the road was jammed with hopeful pilgrims and locals alike. It wasn't hard for the disciples to rouse the crowd—"Jesus has proclaimed himself King!" The multitude laid their cloaks across his path to honor him. They broke branches from the palm trees, waving them in the air and spreading them on the road. This symbolism was actually quite profound.

The last time the Jews had gained independence from the hands of an outside nation was almost 200 years earlier when Judas Maccabeus was made king after liberating Israel from the Syrian empire. On that occasion, he adopted the palm branch as his symbol of victory (1 Maccabees 13:51; 2 Maccabees 10:7). He also put the image of a palm branch on his coins and used them in temple feasts to celebrate the victory over their previous conquerors.

During the Triumphal Entry, when the crowd rushed to get palm branches, it was not just because they were convenient. They envisioned a deliverance similar to the one Judas Maccabeus had provided. That is why the crowd cried "Hosanna", which literally means "Please save!" or "Help!" They wanted help. They wanted to be saved. But saved from what?

After years of Roman occupation, the Jewish people were longing for change. They envisioned a life of greater freedom and an improvement in their standard of living. Things seemed to be falling into place. For much of Jesus' ministry, he had exercised his power solely on the margins of society—the poor, the outcast, the leper, the sinner. But now, he crossed the threshold of the Jewish political center with an entry that would not go unnoticed. Indeed, his arrival was provocative.

The masses were intoxicated with ecstatic frenzy. Others were less impressed.

In Luke's account of the story, the Pharisees responded negatively to the crowd's adulation of Jesus: *"Teacher, rebuke your followers for saying things like that!"* (Luke 19:39) They couldn't believe Jesus was the true Messiah. The religious leaders felt this perception of the Galilean carpenter was inappropriate and liable to stir up more trouble with the Romans. In response to the Pharisee's criticism, Jesus replied, *"I tell you…if they keep quiet, the stones will cry out"* (Luke 19:40 NIV).

Even though they didn't understand his comeback, Jesus upped the ante with his comment—he amplified his claim to power, not just over Jerusalem, but over every aspect of Creation. Yes, he is Lord of even the rocks, but there is more. How about that donkey? If such an animal had never been ridden before, I can't imagine that it would peacefully cooperate unless some supernatural power was involved. Certainly, what Jesus was doing at this point in history had cosmic significance, not just for the people of the world, but for all Creation.

But there is still so much muddled human thinking in this story. Matthew tells us that when Jesus entered Jerusalem, the whole city was stirred and asked, *"Who is this?"* (21:10) That's a good question—who is this Messiah? Or perhaps, more importantly, who is Jesus to me? What kind of a Savior do I really want?

The problem with palms is that once you cut the branches from the tree, they don't live long. The problem with Palm Sunday is that the excitement of the crowd soon faded, and when Good Friday rolled around, some of those same voices that shouted "Hosanna" now shouted "Crucify Him!" Their love for the Lord was shallow, based entirely on their self-centered hope of what he could do for them. There were an abundance of eager pilgrims ready to get behind Jesus on the road to the throne, but they would not follow him on the way to the cross. They would wave palms before the coming king, but they would not obey the Suffering Servant.

So I ask the question again—what kind of Savior are we looking for? What do we really want to be saved from? Chances are, we may not be that different from these first-century Jews. They had their own perception of dire personal need; they knew what they wanted to be delivered from. Perhaps we also have things we want to be delivered from. What do you want to be saved from? It's probably not Roman domination, but how about a bad relational issue? Stress at work? Financial debt? A health problem? Boredom with your life? We all have personal situations that we want to be saved from. You might be saying, "I've had it! Enough already! Hosanna! Jesus, save me! Save me from my problems!"

You know, it's fine to ask Jesus to save us from our problems, but that's not really the point of life. Jesus did not come merely to deliver us from our troubles. Deliverance from personal strains and stresses is not the main idea of the Kingdom God is building, the one established on the death and resurrection of his son.

We are fairly obsessed with our own personal emancipation. We subtly and overtly demand that God fix things for us. Like the children of Israel in AD 30, we may be feeling like the "poor, oppressed people of God who should not have to be in this tough situation…because we are, after all, the people of God." We subconsciously mandate that God make things better for us. We are so very self-centered.

The Kingdom of God, on the other hand, is God-centered. Jesus perfectly modeled God-centeredness in his own life, and is building his church on that principle. And we need to learn to think in this new way. For God's thinking addresses what is truly important.

But like the Jews who witnessed Palm Sunday, many people in the church today do not want the real Jesus either. Instead of embracing the one who came to *"save his people from their sins"* (Matthew 1:21) and the domination of Satan, they're looking for a genie in a bottle. Instead of clinging to the one who can deliver them from death and grant them eternal life, they cheapen God's grace by predominantly desiring health, wealth, and worldly power.

But King Jesus came not to give us the things of this world, but to give us peace with God and peace of mind. Jesus' primary interest is not to make us rich, healthy, powerful, or famous, but to save us from slavery to sin, Satan, and death. Jesus comes not to make the pain go away, but to show us how to live through the pain and chaos in his strength, and to glorify God by our actions. This is a kingdom where bad things happen to good people so the rest of the world gets a chance to see the power of God manifested in our weakness.

Can you hear Jesus speaking to you today? "You know my child, I didn't come just to save you from your problems, but to save you from the domination of sin in your life. I didn't come largely to make your life more comfortable, but to give you strength to be obedient to my holy Father. In this world you will have trouble. But be encouraged, I have overcome the world and I will reward those who are faithful to me. I didn't come to give you Heaven on Earth but to take you safely from Earth to Heaven, so that your redeemed life can glorify God into eternity. I came to give you a cross first, and then a crown."

Two thousand years ago, the Jewish people enthusiastically celebrated their 'Savior'. They cried "Hosanna!" But these people were obsessed with puny human thinking that would bring only a temporary reprieve from something terribly paltry. Jesus, however, came to save them eternally from something much bigger.

What kind of a Savior are you looking for today? What kind of a kingdom do you want? If you want a hero that will take care of all your problems, cheer wildly if you desire, but you're in the wrong ball park.

If you want to be a part of the Kingdom of obedience, of dying to self, of taking up your cross and following Jesus, get ready to polish your trophy. You may not necessarily always feel like a winner now, but one day, the one who came in peace, riding on a donkey, will come again to vindicate his bride, this time riding on a white war horse to battle and conquer all his enemies.

But until that day, "Hosanna" still needs to be cried out by all who are willing to pursue Jesus properly. "Hosanna! Save us Jesus. Save us from our sins, from ourselves, from death. Save us from our selfishness that wants relief more than learning and comfort more than holiness. Hosanna! Lord Jesus, save us!"

DISCUSSION QUESTIONS

1. At first glance, what is odd about the Triumphal Entry?

2. Describe the confused thinking of the Jews surrounding Jesus' entry into Jerusalem the week before he died.

3. Why did Jesus wait so long to publicly proclaim himself as the Messiah and the King?

4. What is the significance of the palm branches in the story?

5. List three ways Jesus demonstrated his power over all Creation in the Triumphal Entry.

6. What does the word 'Hosanna' literally mean?

7. What kind of Savior do we naturally want?

8. What kind of Savior is the real Jesus?

Chapter 18

"My Kingdom is the exact opposite of everything you'd expect."

"Seek the Kingdom of God above all else, and live righteously and he will give you everything you need."

~ Matthew 6:33

Historians love to chew over the age-old question—who was the greatest king to have ever lived? A typical human response begins with calculations of breadth and impact. Great kings build great kingdoms that influence or profoundly change the lives of millions. Who would win the title of greatest monarch ever?

Perhaps it would be Egypt's Khufu who, 4500 years ago, mobilized a myriad of masses to construct a twelve-billion-pound tombstone. Or, Alexander the Great, who inspired men and conquered territory like no other. Maybe it would be Genghis Khan with his masterful ability to unify, organize, and culturally enrich the lives of countless multi-ethnic subjects. Or, how about King Ferdinand of fifteenth-century Spain who initiated the European colonization of the world? And can you pass by Napoleon who, out of ten years of imperial reign, lived only 955 days in Paris and yet totally remade and modernized France?

Regardless of your choice for all-time champion monarch, a human perspective of kings and kingdoms stands in stark contrast to God's Kingdom. The Kingdom of God is so foreign to human contemplation, we need great spiritual enlightenment to pry open its mysteries. Even in Jesus' day, they didn't get it. He was continually confronted with confused thinking about his Father's Kingdom.

Christ's Jewish contemporaries reduced the Kingdom concept to an earthly political empire where God's chosen people, led by their Messiah, would lay a licking on their Roman adversaries. That was as far as their understanding extended. Frankly, God's Kingdom will one day include aspects of divine retribution against the enemies of the Lord; but in the meantime, there is a full Kingdom life to be experienced that has little to do with physical weapons or opulent palaces.

When he appeared on the scene, Jesus proclaimed: *"The Kingdom of God is near!"* (Mark 1:15) His presence made it possible for humans to connect with God in a new way. This personal relationship with the Almighty implied life changes in the present and everlasting life into the future. For at its most basic level, the Kingdom of God is, quite simply, salvation for mankind, eternal life for those who believe and fully commit to following him.

The contrast between God's Kingdom and worldly kingdoms was clear from the beginning. Jesus told his followers: *"My Kingdom is not of this world"* (John 18:36). And yet, his listeners repeatedly struggled to release their minds of earthly notions as the Master taught them about the Kingdom of God. Christ taught that the Kingdom of God is primarily an ethereal kingdom that is assaulting the spiritual reign of Satan by winning the hearts of men and women one at a time (Matthew 12:22–29).

Eventually, God's Kingdom will be fully consummated and will replace every square inch of Satan's current empire. This full fruition of God's reign will be realized not by political or religious movements or any other human intervention, but rather by God himself, at his initiative when judgment is due. And on that day, according to the parable of the sheep and the goats (Matthew 25:31–46), God will differentiate between those who have truly followed him and those who claimed to, but haven't done so.

Unlike human kingdoms where conquest and subjugation are common, God's Kingdom is a kingdom of voluntary subjects who enter by repentance (Matthew 3:1–2), coming from all four corners of the Earth (Luke 13:29). It is a kingdom that is now preached by faithful followers (Luke 9:60) and will continue to be preached until the Second Coming of Christ (Matthew 24:14). And this preaching contains a message of new birth, necessary for relationship with God. Even a pre-converted Apostle Paul, with all his brilliance and training, was unfit for the Kingdom until he was born again.

Entrance to the Kingdom is offered to all, but some have a more difficult time getting in because, as Jesus warned, seekers must be willing to sacrifice everything to cross the threshold, even body parts that may be causing sin (Mark 9:43–48).

The words of Jesus are still challenging today:

> *If you want to be my disciple, you must hate everyone else by comparison—your father and mother, wife and children, brothers and sisters—yes, even your own life. Otherwise, you cannot be my disciple. And if you do not carry your own cross and follow me, you cannot be my disciple...So you cannot become my disciple without giving up everything you own* (Luke 14:26–27, 33).

Accordingly, rich people have a hard time gaining access to the Kingdom because of the enjoyment of wealth (Matthew 19:23–24). In fact, those hoping to enter must do so as a small child, with simplistic faith and unadulterated trust (Matthew 18:1–4; 19:13–15).

And it's no easy task, even for the willing. For Jesus said, *"Work hard to enter the narrow door to God's Kingdom, for many will try to enter but will fail"* (Luke 13:24). But no matter how hard it may be to enter, Jesus assured us that we must be willing to procure access at all costs because the Kingdom (i.e. eternal life) is valuable beyond all description (Matthew 13:44–46).

But who ends up in the Kingdom may be surprising. Jesus tipped off his listeners to the fact that many 'participants' in the Kingdom will actually fail to enter. In the parable of the great supper (Luke 14:15–24), Jesus likened the Kingdom to a sumptuous feast, ready to be enjoyed. Most of the guests on the original invitation list snubbed the banquet call, providing excuses as to why they couldn't attend. Judging by the host's response, Jesus was informing the Jews that their place in the Kingdom would be taken by *"the poor, the crippled, the blind, and the lame"* (Luke 14:21).

Entrance into God's Kingdom depends on the response of the individual. As noted in Jesus' parable of the Pharisee and the tax collector, the Great King wants willing, repentant, and broken hearts, not self-righteous religious practitioners (Luke 18:9–14). Jesus conveyed this message not just through his teaching, but by how he cared for and associated with those whom Jewish society had rejected—he willingly healed the lepers (Luke 17:11–19) and even helped out a Roman centurion (Luke 7:1–10).

This is a kingdom where one human soul is more precious than 2000 animals (Mark 5:1–13). It is a kingdom with ideals diametrically opposed to human thinking. Instead of celebrating regal displays of grandiose strength and ostentatious achievement, God's Kingdom values mourning, meekness, mercy, purity, peace, a hunger for righteousness, and suffering for godly living (Matthew 5:1–12). It is the poor in spirit who will receive the Kingdom. Reputations are left to the care of the Master as all human resource is abandoned to partake in the divine dominion.

God's Kingdom is about what really matters. Religious people debate rituals and practices, but the one true King of the Universe primarily commands holiness. This is exactly what Paul said as well: *"For the Kingdom of God is not a matter of what we eat or drink, but of living a life of goodness and peace and joy in the Holy Spirit"* (Romans 14:17).

And for those wholly committed, the act of seeking God's Kingdom inadvertently supplies all temporal needs. Unlike earthly kingdoms that must concern themselves with providing their own sustenance, members of God's Kingdom are exhorted:

> *Don't worry about these things, saying, "What will we eat? What will we drink? What will we wear?" These things dominate the thoughts of unbelievers, but your heavenly Father already knows all your needs. Seek the Kingdom of God above all else, and live righteously, and he will give you everything you need* (Matthew 6:31–33).

Earthly kingdoms are threatened internally by conspiracy plots and externally by enemy attacks. God's Kingdom is challenged by worry, doubt, and independence from the Creator.

> *That is why I tell you not to worry about everyday life— whether you have enough food and drink, or enough clothes to wear. Isn't life more than food, and your body more than clothing? Look at the birds. They don't plant or harvest or store food in barns, for your heavenly Father feeds them. And aren't you far more valuable to him than they are? Can all your worries add a single moment to your life?* (Matthew 6:25–27)

Earthly kingdoms require strength and ferocity; God's Kingdom demands surrender and faith.

But beyond submission and trust, God's Kingdom advocates the utmost in morality. The ruler of this Kingdom has standards that are higher than any human would set. People living lifestyles of cheating, abuse, greed, drunkenness, idol worship, or sexual immorality will not inherit the Kingdom of God (1 Corinthians 6:9–10; Galatians 5:21).

According to our own understanding, we might feel we are doing pretty well. But in God's Kingdom, perfection is the goal (Matthew 5:48) and the math is demanding—lustful thoughts equals adultery, and careless angry words equals murder (Matthew 5:21–30). And loving only those who are nice to us is just not good enough (Matthew 5:43–47).

Participation in this Kingdom requires great care and respect for others, especially the unlovely and the mean. Sacrificial love appears to be one of its main themes. The parable of the unforgiving servant informs us that we will be judged based on how we have behaved towards others (Matthew 18:21–35). This principle was reinforced in the story of the Good Samaritan (Luke 10:25–37) where Jesus provided an example of a role model for right living in the neighborhood amidst the busy affairs of life. Jesus' coaching to *"love your neighbor as yourself"* (Mark 12:31), stressed the importance God places on our relationships with others.

In contrast to human kingdoms where the eager and ambitious hoard and scheme to get ahead, God's Kingdom provides great gain for those who give things up: *"Whoever wants to be first among you must be the slave of everyone else"* (Mark 10:44). Status perceptions are reversed—the last are first and the first are last (Mark 10:31). The merit-based expectations of effort and reward in earthly kingdoms were blown out of the water by Jesus' parable of the vineyard workers where everybody got the same pay for different amounts of labor (Matthew 20:1–15).

Such teaching was particularly offensive to the religious leaders of the day who expected to assume key positions in God's Kingdom because of their Jewish bloodlines and their hard-earned wealth, intelligence, and positions of authority. The thought of lowly Gentiles taking higher places in the Kingdom was more than they could bear. But that does not diminish the truth—rewards in God's Kingdom are not based on human effort and achievement. There is no rivalry as seen in the usual flurry of human competition. God's Kingdom is clearly a kingdom of grace, where the ruler dispenses his incredible mercies upon his subjects however he pleases.

God's Kingdom is a dominion outside the control of man. It does not grow by human effort, but rather, miraculously by the power of God according to his timing (Mark 4:26–29). It began inconspicuously but promises to develop into something quite prominent (Mark 4:30–32). It is a great entity; but unlike earthly empires, the Kingdom of God can easily be missed by someone lacking spiritual perception. *"The Kingdom of God can't be detected by visible signs. You won't be able to say, 'Here it is!' or 'It's over there!' For the Kingdom of God is already among you"* (Luke 17:20–21).

On one occasion, Jesus equated the Kingdom of God to a seed that is planted in the human heart (Matthew 13:1–23). In order for it to truly flourish there, three things are necessary— understanding, commitment, and total devotion to the Word of God. Without them, the individual slips out of the Kingdom and back into the usual routines of life without God.

However, this Kingdom, no matter how successful, is constantly under attack. The King's loyal subjects are continually challenged by enemies of the realm existing in their midst (Matthew 13:24–43). In fact, according to Christ's teaching, these enemies have been deliberately planted in proximity to the Kingdom as an attempt to sabotage the progress of the Almighty's dominion.

Earthly kingdoms are based on outward appearance. Human empires of all size rely on external image and demonstrations of strength to maintain respect and sustainability. Conversely, Jesus wanted his followers to understand that, in his Father's Kingdom, inner change is far more significant than outward displays of power. He said, *"Don't rejoice because evil spirits obey you; rejoice because your names are registered in heaven"* (Luke 10:20). And God's reign is not pretentiously showy or bombastic like many earthly kingdoms. The Apostle Paul wrote, *"For the Kingdom of God is not just a lot of talk; it is living by God's power"* (1 Corinthians 4:20).

Certainly, Jesus performed many miracles to demonstrate his legitimacy and divine authority in the establishment of God's Kingdom. But the supernatural phenomena were not an end unto themselves; they were a means to a greater end— authenticating the ministry of the one who would die for the sins of the world, allowing humble humans access to the Heavenly Father's Kingdom. Where human kingdoms, historically, have relied on bloodlines to validate and maintain authority, God's Kingdom is based on the shed blood of Jesus on the cross.

Indeed, God is telling us today, "My Kingdom is the exact opposite of everything you'd expect." It's a kingdom of the infirm, the needy, and the broken. Humility will win out over pride, service over status, sacrifice over accumulation, and love over clever schemes. It's a kingdom where the underdog and the oppressed can gain seats of pre-eminence because of the work of Jesus and the grace of God.

We learn little or nothing about God's Kingdom by studying human kingdoms because they are temporal structures of sovereignty, destined for annihilation. God's Kingdom is eternal and will reign supreme over the affairs of men and angels. This Kingdom is present among us today, though very few acknowledge its existence. This proves, once again, that things in this world are not always what they seem. To the naked human eye, equipped with meager natural discernment, earthly kingdoms battle for world supremacy and domination bragging rights. But to the spiritually discerned and repentant seeker, such sovereignty struggles are immaterial, mere distractions from the true reality of a divine spiritual kingdom that is beginning to rule the Universe, the Kingdom of God—the only kingdom that matters.

DISCUSSION QUESTIONS

1. Is there anything truly worthy of admiration in the accomplishments of all the earthly kings of the past?

2. What is the Kingdom of God?

3. What are the basic differences between earthly kingdoms and the Kingdom of God?

4. Who will largely be the recipients of the Kingdom of God in eternity?

5. It's easy to enter the Kingdom of God. Agree or disagree.

6. In your opinion, what are the most perplexing aspects of God's Kingdom?

7. "This is a kingdom where one human soul is more valuable than 2000 animals." Explain.

8. Why did the Jews of Jesus' day have such a hard time accepting his teaching on the Kingdom?

Chapter 19

"It's a home run!"

"Look, God's home is now among his people!
He will live with them, and they will be his people.
God himself will be with them."

~ Revelation 21:3

Our hearts are always hungry for home.
No matter how great the vacation, and regardless of how much fun we've had, as the holiday draws to a close, we want to be home. When little children are lost, confused, or hurt, they just want to go home. After four hours of clothes shopping, I really want to be home.

Home provides us with so many of the things we crave—peace, help, safety, comfort, nourishment, familiarity, love, rest, and recovery. Home is the place where we know the routines and know that we are known. Only in our homes can we kick back, relax, and feel comfortable being ourselves.

Even when homes are abusive, victims yearn for some other version of home where they can secure what they need to cope. Such respite and consolation are often found at a friend's or relative's house, or with someone else experiencing a similar abusive situation.

Because of this common human longing for home, it's reasonable to assume that God has instilled this instinct within us. But, as usual, this God-given desire has been twisted by human thinking.

Instead of hungering to be at home with God, this natural pining for home has turned into a fascination and preoccupation with our earthly houses. Where God has wired us to find all our comfort and security in him, we still believe we might find it in a bigger and nicer home.

We always want to improve our housing situation. Like many before me, I have traveled the path of residential escalation. In the first years of our marriage, Jeanette and I lived in a two-room basement suite. Eventually, we progressed to a two-bedroom apartment followed by an even nicer apartment in a high rise tower. After my university years, we moved to a new town to start my teaching career where we rented a three-bedroom townhouse with a tiny yard. A few years later, we purchased our first single dwelling—a two-and-a-half storey 1912 Victorian home that we enjoyed for twelve years. And now, for the past decade or so, we have lived in a more than ample bungalow nestled in a quaint town in the middle of the Canadian prairies. I couldn't ask for anything more—big yard, five bedrooms, three baths, two large rec rooms, complete with a killer kitchen, oak floors, and French doors.

But guess what I'm doing? The same thing I've been doing all throughout my habitat history—dreaming of the next bigger and better place with more room, nicer wood, greener yard, and more attractive neighborhood. Even though I have a total of 3000 square feet and everything I could possibly need, I still dream of something nicer, newer, and more elegant. Why do we have these impulses?

Granted, often the longing for bigger and better is part of the natural flow of life with children growing in size and number. But with the kids all grown and gone, there is no excuse for my seemingly unquenchable desire for a better home.

God has wired our hearts for home, but our human thinking has twisted this aspiration into something not intended by him. It is human to believe that true security, peace, and comfort can be found in something built by our own hands, our own little castle. We want to make ourselves happy and safe by our own doing. We find it hard to trust God to supply all that we need. And so we continue to hunt for that perfect home. Instead of seeing our true home as an intimate abiding with God, we vainly chase real estate ads and foolishly dream of Hollywood mansions.

Such warped human judgment has been prevalent throughout all of history. Those of us with the means rarely miss the opportunity to build ourselves an extravagant mansion. From the most ancient civilizations until this day, humans have constructed massive dwelling places and filled them with creaturely comforts to satisfy our powerful urges to be secure and at ease.

Ancient Egyptians even carried this obsession into the afterlife. Powerful pharaohs built great pyramids as homes for their final resting places. The labor involved in those colossal stone structures on the plains of Giza is unparalleled in effort and ingenuity.

In the seventh century B.C., the Babylonian King Nebuchadnezzar built himself a spectacular new palace, complete with hanging gardens that came to be revered as one of the seven wonders of the ancient world. Like all of us, Nebuchadnezzar couldn't resist ogling over all he had built.

Twelve months later he was taking a walk on the flat roof of the royal palace in Babylon. As he looked out across the city, he said, "Look at this great city of Babylon! By my own mighty power, I have built this beautiful city as my royal residence to display my majestic splendor" (Daniel 4:29–30).

The later verses of this passage tell the story of how God straightened out Nebuchadnezzar's thinking, but it was a wild humbling ride necessitated by foolish notions of self-sufficiency and extravagant house design.

For centuries, European aristocrats and monarchs built huge castles to fortify themselves, show off their wealth, and glorify their own perceived greatness. Some mansions, like Louis XIV's Palace at Versailles, were constructed in such a fashion as to tell elaborate stories of personal and national greatness. The Sun King's architectural masterpiece was an allegory of his own persona, with all the rooms surrounding his second floor bedroom named after planets in the Solar System. All staircases led to Louis' bedroom where visitors could watch the sun rise (awake) and set (go to bed) on a daily basis. The long-reigning French monarch saw himself as eternal, so he built an unfathomably opulent residence worthy of his majesty and supremacy.

Versailles' masterful design gave the illusion of security, but as Louis XVI would find out one hundred years later, France's greatest palace provided very little protection from the angry mobs of the French Revolution.

Windsor Castle in Berkshire, England, is another prime example of going over the top. Originally built by William the Conqueror and remodeled over centuries, this British monarch residence has 1000 rooms sprawled over 484 000 square feet of floor space situated on a modest thirteen acres of land. Currently, it is the largest dwelling place in the world.

Of course, even Queen Elizabeth's weekend home dwarfs in comparison to the design and technology of the enigmatic and mind-boggling Washington home of multi-billionaire Bill Gates. In this humble abode,

> ...guests wear pins that upon entrance of a room automatically adjust temperature, music, and lighting based on the guest's preferences. In 2009, property taxes on the home were reported to be US $1.063 million on a total assessed value of US $147.5 million.[25]

---

[25] Cited June 10, 2010 http://en.wikipedia.org/wiki/Bill_Gates'_house

We often build great homes for all the wrong reasons—prestige, status, personal pleasure. Mistakenly we may associate our homes with our identities and self-worth. Humans continually compare houses in a form of ego-based competition where our dwelling places become status symbols of personal wealth and achievement, of having arrived. And, especially during times of economic downturn, our glorious homes can end up trapping us in a financial vice of enormous squeeze. It's stunning how we will subject ourselves to insane mortgages in an effort to try and keep up. Truly, homes often end up owning us.

Humans have placed far too much emphasis on the significance of earthly homes. But God doesn't. Houses may be a general necessity, but our Creator did not intend for us to become as consumed with the matter as we have, especially in the West.

Many biblical characters spent a great deal of their lives without a fixed residence—Abraham, Isaac, Jacob, Moses, David, many of the prophets, as well as several New Testament Apostles (Hebrews 11:9, 38; 1 Corinthians 4:11). As the children of Israel wandered in the wilderness, living in portable tents, they received their comfort and security from the presence of God who dwelt in the Tabernacle (2 Samuel 7:6).

When the Israelites were about to enter the Promised Land, God said they would soon inherit cities and houses they did not build. But he said it in such a matter-of-fact fashion. Simple story—the wickedness of the Canaanites had to be judged, God drove them out, and he gave their houses to his chosen people. Perhaps God did it this way so the Israelites would see these homes as his provision, and not get hung up on proudly building their own little castles of false security.

After all, it was godly obedience and dependence upon the Lord that would maintain the Israelites' security in the Promised Land, not their homes. The point of Israel's existence was to be a light to the nations and to glorify the one true God of the Universe. In time, however, the Israelites got so settled in their homes, enjoying the wealth of the land, that they forgot the Lord and did not respect his land Sabbath regulations. They pushed on for increased prosperity, and desired less and less of God and his presence in their lives. Eventually, God had enough; he removed them from their homes and deposited them in a foreign land where they lived as captives for seventy years.

Even when they returned to their homeland generations later, the Israelites still failed to get their priorities straight, and it cost them dearly. *"You hoped for rich harvests, but they were poor. And when you brought your harvest home, I blew it away. Why? Because my house lies in ruins, says the Lord of Heaven's Armies, while all of you are busy building your own fine houses"* (Haggai 1:9). Any time our homes take precedence over the presence of God in our lives, we are losing out.

The New Testament encourages us to hold on to our houses with loose fingers. In the Gospels, Jesus assured us that no one ever loses out by leaving their home for the sake of the Kingdom of God. Rewards for that kind of sacrifice materialize both now and in eternity (Mark 10:29–30; Luke 18:29–30).

Indeed, our homes should be places of praising God for his good work in our lives (Luke 5:24–25) and declaring to others how much he has done for us (Luke 8:39). They should also be places where Jesus is welcomed (Luke 10:38), truths of God are explained (Acts 18:26 NIV), and Christian hospitality is provided (Hebrews 13:2; 3 John 5). It was very common for the early church to meet in each other's homes for worship (Philemon 1:2) and to partake of the Lord's Supper (Acts 2:46).

But there is no indication in the Scriptures that we should become enamored with our earthly residences. When Christ walked this Earth, he made no attempt to secure a home of his own (Matthew 8:20). Early in the morning, when most of his followers were still reclining in the comfort of their own beds in their homes, Jesus rose to pray, entering into the fellowship of his father to enjoy his presence.

This seems to be the true meaning of 'being home' in the Scriptures—enjoying God's presence. The apostles talked this way. Paul referred to physical death as being *"at home with the Lord"* (2 Corinthians 5:6–8). Peter said, Jesus *"died for sinners to bring you safely home to God"* (1 Peter 3:18).

The story of mankind started in a garden and ends with the New Jerusalem, both elegant sounding habitations. But even in Eden, the emphasis seemed to be more on fellowship with God than on a specific residence for the first humans. I would venture to say that the best part of garden life for Adam and Eve was getting to meet with God regularly in the cool of the day, just to hang out with him and chat. One can only imagine what they talked about every night. And so, when Adam and Eve sinned, the greatest tragedy of their punishment was their banishment from the garden and God's company, and their disqualification from partaking of the good gifts God had given them there (Genesis 3:23–24).

The story of salvation is one of reconciling man back to God (2 Corinthians 5:18–21), where we can, once again, enjoy his presence and blessing in our lives. The point of life has nothing to do with a wild goose chase for that illusive and perfect earthly home.

When the story of mankind draws to a close in Heaven, again we see very little emphasis on personal dwelling arrangements and total focus on the presence of God. The Apostle John writes:

> *Then I saw a new heaven and a new earth, for the old heaven and the old earth had disappeared. And the sea was also gone. And I saw the holy city, the new Jerusalem, coming down from God out of heaven like a bride beautifully dressed for her husband. I heard a loud shout from the throne, saying, "Look, God's home is now among his people! He will live with them, and they will be his people. God himself will be with them. He will wipe every tear from their eyes, and there will be no more death or*

sorrow or crying or pain. All these things are gone forever"
(Revelation 21:1–4).

When we want to determine an author's main idea, we look at the end of the book. The concept of 'fellowship with God' as being the true nature of 'being home' seems quite evident in the Book of Revelation. God wants to dwell amidst his people in perfect fellowship, taking care of all our sorrows and cares. In eternity, God will satisfy every thirst (Revelation 21:6), protect us like his children (Revelation 21:7), and personally take the place of any temple building (Revelation 21:22). He and his son will illuminate every corner of the New Jerusalem by their glorious presence (Revelation 21:23) and nations will walk in this light (Revelation 21:24).

The author of Revelation goes on to say:

> *Then the angel showed me a river with the water of life, clear as crystal, flowing from the throne of God and of the Lamb. It flowed down the center of the main street. On each side of the river grew a tree of life, bearing twelve crops of fruit, with a fresh crop each month. The leaves were used for medicine to heal the nations. No longer will there be a curse upon anything. For the throne of God and of the Lamb will be there, and his servants will worship him. And they will see his face, and his name will be written on their foreheads. And there will be no night there—no need for lamps or sun—for the Lord God will shine on them. And they will reign forever and ever* (Revelation 22:1–5).

In my childhood, I was told regularly that God has a lavish mansion waiting for me in Heaven. In church, we sang about it—*"I've got a mansion, just over the hilltop"*. Such a perspective may encourage us to miss the point. I believe we have mistakenly emphasized the mansion aspect of Heaven because of the way the King James Version translated John 14:2—*"In my Father's house are many mansions"*. Years of reciting this version have left a mark on my psyche. The connotation of mansion is one of lavish and palatial splendor, but the Greek word used by John in this verse simply means a dwelling, room, or abode.[26]

Christ had something important to say in John 14. God's beloved children will one day be with Christ in his home. Jesus was talking with his disciples about going away. This news obviously disturbed them; they couldn't imagine life without their friend. Jesus wanted to ease their troubled hearts, so he used the image of a Jewish man going off to prepare a place in his father's house for his new bride. When the addition was ready, the bridegroom would come and retrieve his bride and take her to their new home where she would dwell securely with her lover.

Jesus did not say to his disciples: "Don't be troubled; you'll be rich one day with a fabulous palace to live in." Rather, he said, "Don't worry, some day, when the time is right, we will be together again…forever." *"When everything is ready, I will come and get you, so that you will always be with me where I am"* (John 14:3).

To 'be home' means to be with Jesus and his father in Heaven, eternally. And such a homecoming is not reserved solely for the afterlife. Later in the same passage Jesus explained that we can be at home spiritually right now. *"All who love me will do what I say. My Father will love them, and we will come and make our home with each of them"* (John 14:23). He finished with these encouraging words: *"I am leaving you with a gift—peace of mind and heart. And the peace I give is a gift the world cannot give. So don't be troubled or afraid. Remember what I told you: I am going away, but I will come back to you again"* (John 14:27–28a).

Everlasting fellowship with our Heavenly Father and his son—that is our destiny as believers. That is what it means to be home. That is what our hearts are truly hungering for. Sadly, we confuse this urge with the human desire to acquire a better place to live, one that will supposedly satisfy our souls.

---

[26] F. Wilbur Gingrich, *Shorter Lexicon of the Greek New Testament* (Chicago: The University of Chicago Press, 1965) p. 140

To think like a human is to miss the point and crave for an earthly mansion. To think like God is to use our homes as places of Christian service, all the while knowing that our true place of peace, safety, and security lies within the arms of the Almighty Living God. As Moses wrote in Psalm 90:1, *"Lord, through all the generations you have been our home!"*

DISCUSSION QUESTIONS

1. What does 'home' provide for the human soul?

2. Instead of hungering for our eternal home, what do we typically pine for?

3. How has this tendency (#2) been exemplified throughout history?

4. Why do we tend to place so much significance on our earthly homes?

5. What is the biblical teaching on earthly homes?

6. What does the Bible say or imply about us truly 'being home'?

7. What was Jesus really saying in John 14 when he told his disciples about what he was preparing for them?

8. As we reflect on our attitudes toward our earthly homes, what adjustments need to be made in our thinking to align our minds with God's?

Chapter 20

"Are you dying to meet me?"

*"Hard choice! The desire to break camp here
and be with Christ is powerful. Some days
I can think of nothing better."*

~ Philippians 1:23 MSG

Every once in a while, it really hits me—just how far my thinking is from God's. I was reminded of this fact again in January 2010 when Jeanette and I heard that our oldest daughter had been diagnosed with cancer—Hodgkin's lymphoma.

In no uncertain terms, in the face of mortal danger, the Apostle Paul boldly stated, *"For me, to live is Christ, and to die is gain"* (Philippians 1:21 NIV). If I were honest, and spoke my true feelings out loud, I might be heard to say, "For me, to live is to have lots of good friends, happy family memories, and a bunch of cool stuff—and to die is a bummer." When I compare what Paul said to what I might say in a moment of weakness or vulnerability, I would conclude that one of us is psychotic, detached from reality. My guess is that person is not Paul.

We have a difficult time fathoming our death. We often accuse young people of deceptively believing in their own immortality; but even as we get older, it's hard to grasp death.

How is it that we have become so disconnected from the truth regarding matters of life and death? Why do we hunger more for an earthly home than a heavenly one? Why is it so hard to genuinely look forward to Heaven, with absolutely no fear of death?

Certainly, an unbeliever's fear of death subjects him or her to a life of bondage (Hebrews 2:15). As a concrete floor awaits a falling light bulb, the faithless one awaits with horror the Grim Reaper's call. All that is left for unbelievers is to grab all the gusto they can.

Not so for followers of Jesus Christ. Or, at least, it shouldn't be. But even Christians who have devoted their lives to Christ can struggle with selfishness in the face of death, as if the sorrow of impending departure establishes the prerogative to be self-centered, to turn inward.

Instead of using their 'valley of the shadow of death' to glorify God and eagerly anticipate their union with Christ, some believers are engulfed in thoughts of pity—"Poor me", "I'm too young", "I haven't done everything yet that I wanted to accomplish in life", "Why does this have to happen to me?", "It's not fair". That first night when we heard the news about our daughter, I myself said to Jeanette, "This can't be right. She's too young to be facing this!"

We talk about living for Christ, but what about dying for him? News of a fatal or potentially fatal illness often slides us into depression and despair. If we are children of God, why does the prospect of death make us so sad? As Christians, can we not experience some form of miraculous joy in the face of mortal illness, knowing that the one who is passing will soon be with the Lord, reunited with loved ones who have gone on before? As a believer, certainly, *"to be absent from the body"*…is…*"to be present with the Lord"* (2 Corinthians 5:8 KJV).

Why do we act like this world is the main prize and Heaven is just the consolation? When our favorite beauty pageant contestant fails to win the crown, we console ourselves in the fact, "Well, at least she won Miss Congeniality." I've heard Christians say regarding the death of a fellow believer, "Well, at least we know he's in Heaven now." This makes it sound like the main point of life is to have an earthly existence that is as long as possible until we finally cave in and are forced to go to Heaven.

This kind of worldly thinking makes me wonder if we truly believe in Heaven—I mean *really* believe. We say we believe in it, but why do we struggle to live out that belief? Why is the concept of God's glorious Heaven so foreign to our daily grind worldview? Perhaps it's because we mistakenly perceive life as merely a mundane grind instead of a celebrated journey to Heaven.

Believers who die young need to be seen as the lucky ones who attain a shortcut to our ultimate destiny. Of course, I'm not condoning suicide, and it makes perfect sense to try to survive in the face of danger and illness since God has built this into our instincts. But when the Lord declares that his faithful child's time is up, we need to consider this a victory, not a defeat. That person has won the gold medal, not just the silver or the bronze.

Perhaps our Savior is standing at the pearly gates, asking the question of us, "Are you dying to meet me?"

After all, we're all dying. It's just a matter of time until this earthly tent collapses. And only in death will we recognize how restricting and limiting our earthly bodies have been. Where we once saw a few threads, we will view the whole tapestry. Where we once saw only a few walls of the maze, we will see the entire city.

One of the few certain things in life is death. But a believer needs to see death for what it truly is—a new birth. For those who have been made right with God by the blood of Jesus, physical death is the passageway that launches us into the final stage of life. Our bodies and clothes may stay in the coffin, but we will not be there. We will be with the Lord.

Ironically, today's medical advancements often prolong survival, extending the no-holds-barred death journey, as the patient endures months of experimental therapies and painful treatments. Years ago, fatal illnesses swept away their victims briskly. Modern medicine has inadvertently often increased the suffering of our earthly bodies' final stages.

But in eternity, we will look back and wonder what all the fuss was about during our short stay in our limited bodies. We will chuckle at our miniscule perspective like an amused father who listens to the confused philosophies of a three-year-old trying to understand how a baby can live in mommy's tummy.

But one cannot address this matter without the risk of causing offense. Those who have walked the dark valley of losing a dear loved one are all too familiar with deep sadness. Certainly, those who have experienced a fatal tragedy find it hard to process the event purely through a logical lens, apart from emotions. For it is death's sting of sorrow that consumes our souls in the dark hours of the night—loneliness, disappointment, regret, unresolved anger, unfinished adventures, unfulfilled potential, and orphaned children.

To the young mother left with three small children, how can a husband's untimely death be seen as anything but horrifically tragic? The sick feeling of being punched in the stomach will not easily dissipate. The absence of something so precious tastes like famine. The disappearance of someone so valued feels like drought.

As comforters to our grief-stricken friends, the worst thing we can be in these moments of loss is trite. People don't need pat answers. And they don't need to be told that what they're experiencing will be good for them. The Wonderful Counselor wants to comfort us in our sorrows, and we as caregivers need to mimic that behavior.

But that does not mean we abandon the truth. At some point in the grieving process, we need to acknowledge that life is bigger than our bodies, bigger than our families, and bigger than our world. True life is a relationship with God, both now and into eternity.

Earth is the breeding ground and the practice stage for the real performance. That's it. No more. We're here preparing for the next phase. Earthly goals with no heavenly connection are pointless. When we deceive ourselves into thinking that a solid retirement plan is the main point of life, we are totally missing the point.

When we think human thoughts about death, and sadly cling to earthly life as the sole prize, we are like unborn babies who are enjoying the comforts of the womb, afraid of the unknown accompanying the next step. Though the child may not want to leave his familiar surroundings, the parents know that he has not yet even begun to live.

And we, laying on our death beds, are tempted to cling to the last vestiges of 'life', when, in reality, true life is only about to begin. Tiny human thinking sees death as the final wrap-up, the last curtain call. Thinking like God sees our Heavenly Father cheering on his kids, telling them to get their shoes on because the game is about to begin.

Theologically, we need to understand that death for believers is the bell that signals the start of the party. Practically speaking, death usually feels likes the party is over.

Even Jesus wept when he encountered his friends mourning the death of Lazarus. I often wonder why Jesus cried at this event. Was he expressing his humanness, agonizing over the death of a dear friend? Was he just moved by the sadness of the others? Was he distressed that no one, even Martha and Mary, believed that he could actually raise Lazarus back to life? Surely he wasn't broken-hearted that Lazarus was dead because he knew he was going to remedy that situation in a few minutes. Perhaps he was sad that his friends were so consumed with a worldly perspective.

Regardless of the reason for his tears, we learn something about the thoughts of God through Jesus' behavior in this story. The main idea of the miracle was not to raise up Lazarus so he could live eternally in his original body. No, he died later anyway. And the main point was not just to make everyone happy. Jesus said the point of the miracle was to bring glory to God, demonstrate the Lord's almighty power, and help people believe in him as the Christ (John 11:4, 15, 40, 42, 45).

Helping people in this world get connected with Jesus is a significant component of the journey. After all, Jesus is the determining factor in the type of eternity to be experienced by each and every human. Those aspects of Creation that are reconciled back to God through the blood of Jesus eagerly await to be released from their prison of earthly boundaries. Once released, there will not be the slightest thought of wanting to ever return back to an earlier existence.

Perhaps Paul Young was trying to communicate this truth in *The Shack*. Yes, Missy's kidnapping and murder were dreadful events. But when Mack sees his little girl playing by the brook in fields of beautiful foliage in the warmth of Jesus' love, 'The Great Sadness' lifts. Why would he want his daughter back in this world of sickness and pain?[27]

Why do we desire to have our loved ones back? Why would we want them to be absent from the Lord and present with us, back in an aching and faulty flesh container? Who are we thinking about primarily as we grieve in this way?

When witnessing an anguished family or a group of friends accompanying someone in their last days, it's apparent that the one dying is usually the bravest. If that individual is a believer, true reality is starting to kick in. What before was reality is now becoming a dream. What before was a dream is now becoming reality. Eternity is becoming the genuine article, and earthly life, the shadow. The earth-centered temporal life now seems like some crazy illusion that was foolishly chased for years.

Yes, things are starting to get clearer for the one who is staring death in the face. Unfortunately, mourning loved ones will be left to meander in the fog of what feels like unfinished journeys.

---

[27] William P. Young, *The Shack*. (Los Angeles, CA: Windblown Media, 2007)

Acts 7 records the final words of Stephen as he was being stoned to death by an angry mob. He prayed, *"'Lord Jesus, receive my spirit.' He fell to his knees, shouting, 'Lord, don't charge them with this sin!'"* (59–60) Because he was in right relationship with God, Stephen was perfectly comfortable passing from this world into the presence of his Savior.

The eternal life we receive through Christ Jesus is not just about longevity. It's a quality of life that starts from the moment he delivers us from the power of sin's hold on our lives (Romans 6:6). Living richly in that communion with the Lord throughout our earthly days makes it easier to move into his presence at death's door.

Personally, I want to live for Christ. But when the time comes, I hope also to die for him. I hope I don't become focused on myself and solely preoccupied with deliverance from the dark valley. I hope I don't feel sorry for myself. I hope I don't fail to glorify God. I hope I don't embarrass my Savior who died for me. Just as I taught my children how to live, I hope I show them how to die.

If I fail, if my conversation begins to display self-centered thoughts instead of thoughts of God's goodness and faithfulness, I may nullify everything I have lived for. Such behavior might even convince some onlookers that I didn't actually believe in Jesus in the first place. That would be tragic.

At this point you might be thinking, "Okay. This perspective on death is fine for the one dying, but what about the ones left behind? What about the sorrow experienced by the survivors, especially if there are young children in the story who may have to go through the rest of their lives without mother or father?"

Fair question. How does God expect the survivors to handle their loss and go on with strength and courage?

Certainly not with denial. There is no value in hiding from the pain of searing loss. I understand we must let the tragic event run its course in our human emotions. But that pain need not lead to total discouragement and disillusionment.

It is, after all, primarily a matter of trust. Do we trust God? Do we believe he is good, even though he did not stop a bad thing from happening? Do we believe he loves us when things have gone awry? Do we believe that the loving arms of God never failed to embrace our loved ones as they passed from this world to the next?

When we walk with the Lord, our earthly demise is really a graduation, a celebration of the victory that Christ has won over the sting of death. At this point, we enter into perfect fellowship with the triune God who loved us even before the foundation of the world. And truly, *"No eye has seen, no ear has heard, and no mind has imagined what God has prepared for those who love him"* (1 Corinthians 2:9).

And for people of faith, miracles can even happen here on Earth in the midst of the tragedy. Hardship can be turned to hope and travesty to triumph. God has promised to be *"a father to the fatherless, a defender of widows"* (Psalm 68:5 NIV). I have seen this truth exhibited in my wife's family. Even though the Lord allowed her husband to die of leukemia at the age of twenty-nine, Jeanette's mom has maintained her pure and simple faith in the Lord. Even though she had three young sons and was pregnant with Jeanette at the time, she refused to let bitterness envelop her soul. She carried on with life, raising a family to love and respect the God of Creation who gives and takes away according to his sovereign plan (Job 1:21).

She honored the life of her husband who is, at this moment, *"alive with Christ"* (Colossians 2:13). We tend to think of this phrase as referring solely to being spiritually alive versus being spiritually dead. But it's richer and deeper than that. Once we have been made alive by Christ, eternal life has already begun. And mortal death does not truncate it. This is why Jesus said to the religious leaders of his day, *"Long after Abraham, Isaac, and Jacob had died, [Moses] referred to the Lord as 'the God of Abraham, the God of Isaac, and the God of Jacob.' So he is the God of the living, not the dead, for they are all alive to him"* (Luke 20:37–38).

Saints who have gone before us are all now alive, not dead. Today, Peter and Paul are alive. Stephen is alive. Mary, the mother of Jesus, is alive. Any of our loved ones who have died in the Lord are now alive. Maybe we should take more time to think about this simple concept. Perhaps it would help transform our thinking and put physical death in its proper perspective.

It also helps to examine the experience of others before us who have faced the shadow of death. The Scriptures offer several poignant examples of both proper and improper responses to our earthly exit.

Contrast Moses with Hezekiah when God informed each of them that they were about to die. Instead of pouting or complaining when God said his number was up, Moses stayed focused on the Kingdom of God and the needs of the children of Israel who would now have to go on without him. He said,

> *O Lord, you are the God who gives breath to all creatures. Please appoint a new man as leader for the community. Give them someone who will guide them wherever they go and will lead them into battle, so the community of the Lord will not be like sheep without a shepherd* (Numbers 27:16–17).

And as a point of interest, Moses was not a crotchety old man when he said these things. Scripture says, *"Moses was 120 years old when he died, yet his eyesight was clear, and he was as strong as ever"* (Deuteronomy 34:7).

Hezekiah, on the other hand, wept like a baby at the news of his impending death. Instead of humbly submitting himself to the Lord's timing, he cried out to God for more time until he was granted an extra fifteen years. And we all know how badly that story turned out.

Yes, we are loved by God, but we are not indispensible to his work on Earth. When we die, God will raise up others to do his work and continue to build his church. When Moses passed away, God simply said to Joshua, *"Moses my servant is dead. Therefore, the time has come for you to lead these people, the Israelites, across the Jordan River into the land I am giving them"* (Joshua 1:2). Moses is dead, get busy with what needs to be done. Yes, we mourn and grieve, but not as people without hope. Our dear departed one has gone to glory ahead of us. The work of the Lord carries on.

Following Moses' example, Joshua himself was able to keep his focus clear during his dying years. He gathered the leaders of Israel together and told them, *"I am now a very old man. You have seen everything the Lord your God has done for you during my lifetime. The Lord your God has fought for you against your enemies"* (Joshua 23:2–3). Even as he is about to pass on, Joshua's dying remarks were centered on the faithfulness of God, not on himself. He said, *"Soon I will die, going the way of everything on earth. Deep in your hearts you know that every promise of the Lord your God has come true. Not a single one has failed!"* (Joshua 23:14)

Consider also the gracious manner in which the biblical character Ruth handled her deep suffering and loss. She attended to the needs of others (namely her widowed mother-in-law), valued remaining relationships, and committed herself to living a holy and respectful life before God. The key aspects were that she stayed productive and did not let herself become bitter.

When the advisers of King David questioned him as to why he was doing so well soon after the death of his son through Bathsheba,

David replied, "I fasted and wept while the child was alive, for I said, 'Perhaps the Lord will be gracious to me and let the child live.' But why should I fast when he is dead? Can I bring him back again? I will go to him one day, but he cannot return to me" (2 Samuel 12:22–23).

I applaud David for stating the obvious because we so often miss the obvious. We cannot bring our loved ones back and we are not invincible. We all have an appointment with our Maker. For some, it is sooner than others. Consider brothers James and John in the Gospels—one was beheaded in A.D. 44 while the other lived for another fifty-six years.[28]

Length of years is immaterial. We need to see things from God's perspective. Facing imminent death, David exhorted his son Solomon to

> ...learn to know the God of your ancestors intimately. Worship and serve him with your whole heart and a willing mind. For the Lord sees every heart and knows every plan and thought. If you seek him, you will find him. But if you forsake him, he will reject you forever (1 Chronicles 28:9).

Jesus said, don't fear death; instead, fear God who has the power to kill you and then throw you into hell (Luke 12:5). Back to my own family story...we were overjoyed to watch our daughter face her chemo and radiation appointments with a simple yet strong faith in God. Because of her own personal and vibrant relationship with the Lord, she clearly demonstrated to us that she was prepared to die. Fortunately for us as parents, her treatments were successful and God has blessed her with more time, for now. But we all need to remember this fact—death is not the enemy. Our true enemy is selfish independence from God. That's what we need to watch out for. A life apart from God will earn us an eternal death apart from him.

The Apostle Paul knew this so well. Consider his admonition to his friends shortly before he was put in jail near the end of his life. His friends warned him not to go back to Jerusalem where hateful enemies abounded. They feared that harm would come to their friend Paul. They begged him not to go there.

In response, Paul said,

---

[28] Cited September 13, 2009 http://www.ccel.org/bible/phillips/ CN610CHRONO.htm

Why all this hysteria? Why do you insist on making a scene and making it even harder for me? You're looking at this backward. The issue in Jerusalem is not what they do to me, whether arrest or murder, but what the Master Jesus does through my obedience. Can't you see that? (Acts 21:13 MSG)

It helps when we understand the main point of life. It's not about the bad or hard things that may happen to us; it's about what Jesus can do *through* us, through our obedience to him. Understanding this truth puts our physical death in its proper perspective, as we see the brevity of earthly life and begin to comprehend the glory of eternal life with our wonderful Savior. Perhaps today you can hear the Savior asking, "Are you dying to meet me?"

DISCUSSION QUESTIONS

1. How can Christians be selfish in the face of death?

2. How do we mistakenly portray to the world that Heaven is only a consolation, not the top prize?

3. For a Christian, what is the irony in modern medical advancements?

4. How are we as believers in this world similar to unborn babies in the womb?

5. Why did Jesus cry at Lazarus' tomb?

6. How does God expect the survivors to handle the loss of loved ones?

7. Contrast Moses' and Hezekiah's attitudes towards their impending deaths.

8. How can the Apostle Paul's life and teaching help us to put our earthly demise in its proper perspective?

Conclusion

Jesus came to Earth to do the most significant work in the Universe. All of Creation had to be redeemed from its fallen state, bought back by his blood. In Sunday school terms, Jesus came to die for our sin and to rise again for our resurrection unto new life. Theologically, this divine sacrifice has the power to make us into new creatures (2 Corinthians 5:17). Practically, this total life transformation begins with a renovation of our minds (Romans 12:2). We will not become new people if we hold on to our old thoughts.

Innately, we see things from such a limited vantage point. When we face a tough challenge, all we can muster in our natural state is a human evaluation of the situation. Jesus constantly addressed this problem throughout his earthly ministry. Near the end of his time, when he began to tell his friends that he was going to Jerusalem to die, Peter pulled him aside and rebuked the Savior for what he considered to be confused thinking. Christ responded to his bold companion by saying, *"Get away from me, Satan! You are a dangerous trap to me. You are seeing things merely from a human point of view, not from God's"* (Matthew 16:23).

This will forever be our greatest challenge as we walk through our earthly journeys—to see things from God's point of view when the human perspective seems so tempting, so natural. But just because it's difficult does not mean we should shy away from the challenge. No, in fact, we must continue to work towards this necessary mind renovation.

Everything begins with the brain. The root of, and solution to, every problem lies in the mind. And in our natural state, we have no other source but a fallen human outlook nourished by an evil worldly system. This worldliness—the lust of the flesh, lust of the eyes, and the boastful pride of life—must be yanked out like a cracked old toilet and pitched in the dumpster. Like a shiny new fixture, a divine paradigm must be carefully installed in its place. And the work to be done must not be seen as a weekend project. No. The reconstruction will be an ongoing undertaking. We have to let God's Word speak freely, freshly, and regularly into our lives so that the renovation can be realized. We need to embrace our Savior and his work on the cross. He alone will be able to walk us through the mess. And we must never cease to root out the parts of our thinking that are faulty and frail so they can be replaced.

But most of all, we need to understand and truly believe the personal and spiritual dangers of harboring harmful human thoughts. This is not an optional repair. For when we comfortably embrace our natural human thinking rather than pursuing a mind renovation towards the divine, we, like Peter in his moment of weakness, are actually embracing Satan, hardly a proper or intelligent choice for people who have been *"rescued...from the kingdom of darkness and transferred...into the Kingdom of his dear Son"* (Colossians 1:13).